In this marvellous collection of pithy essays, an international cast of scholars and clinicians endeavour to probe into the multi-layered phenomenon of jealousy. Illustrating their arguments with clinical case-vignettes and examples from popular culture, they demonstrate persuasively that jealousy is not a unitary, monolithic experience, but a complex, composite, and protean aspect of the human mind, which cannot be detached from the social bond. If this book does not make you jealous of the authors' agility and their sparkling insights, it is guaranteed to change your perspective on everything you thought you knew about one of the core components of the human condition.

Dany Nobus, *Professor of Psychoanalytic Psychology,*
Brunel University of London

Lacanian Perspectives on Jealousy

A great effort has been made in contemporary Western culture to move beyond jealousy in our private lives – we have renegotiated old prohibitions, reorganising our sex lives, relationships, and family structures in new and inventive ways. But have we really been so successful at bearing the knowledge that, at a certain point, others' desires belong only to them?

This collection takes the temperature of jealousy today – how does it show up in the clinic? Does this differ from how it used to? What can be said of how jealousy functions both psychically and socially? Clinicians and writers working from within a Lacanian psychoanalytic framework explore the concept and unpack not only its numerous guises and forms, but its founding effects on the levels of both the individual and the social. The question as to where jealousy is located today leads to a deeper look at the feeling's origins: its close relation to identification and with envy, its interaction with early infantile complexes, its constant interplay with the social realm and its systems of governance, and its complex expression of ambivalence towards the maternal.

This book is for anyone interested in psychoanalysis, be they readers or historians of psychoanalysis, or clinicians looking for ways to approach jealousy in their practice. It is also for anyone who knows what it is to suffer jealousy, which, if Freud was right, is most of us.

Carmen Wright is a psychoanalyst and psychotherapist practicing in London. She is a member of the Centre for Freudian Analysis and Research, where she also teaches. She welcomes at the François Dolto–inspired 'Maison Verte' in London, Bubble & Speak.

The Centre for Freudian Analysis and Research Library (CFAR)

Series Editors: Anouchka Grose, Darian Leader, Kristina Valendinova

CFAR was founded in 1985 with the aim of developing Freudian and Lacanian psychoanalysis in the UK. Lacan's rereading and rethinking of Freud had been neglected in the Anglophone world, despite its important implications for the theory and practice of psychoanalysis. Today, this situation is changing, with a lively culture of training groups, seminars, conferences, and publications.

CFAR offers both introductory and advanced courses in psychoanalysis, as well as a clinical training programme in Lacanian psychoanalysis. It can provide access to Lacanian psychoanalysts working in the UK and has links with Lacanian groups across the world. The CFAR Library aims to make classic Lacanian texts available in English for the first time, as well as publishing original research in the Lacanian field.

What Can We Know About Sex?
A Lacanian Study of Sex and Gender
Gisèle Chaboudez

What Does It Mean to Make Love?
A Psychoanalytic Study of Sexuality and Phantasy
Gérard Pommier

How Does Analysis Work?
Examples of Lacanian Interpretation
Edited by Berjanet Jazani

Lacanian Perspectives on Jealousy
Carmen Wright

www.cfar.org.uk
www.routledge.com/The-Centre-for-Freudian-Analysis-and-Research-Library/book-series/KARNACCFARL

Lacanian Perspectives on Jealousy

Edited by Carmen Wright

Routledge
Taylor & Francis Group

LONDON AND NEW YORK

Designed cover image: Cover image © Gabriella Boyd.
All Rights Reserved 2024.

First published 2026
by Routledge
4 Park Square, Milton Park, Abingdon, Oxon OX14 4RN

and by Routledge
605 Third Avenue, New York, NY 10158

Routledge is an imprint of the Taylor & Francis Group, an informa business

British Library Cataloguing-in-Publication Data
A catalogue record for this book is available from the British Library

Library of Congress Cataloging-in-Publication Data
Names: Wright, Carmen (Psychoanalyst) editor
Title: Lacanian perspectives on jealousy / edited by Carmen Wright.
Description: Abingdon, Oxon ; New York, NY : Routledge, 2026. | Series: The Centre for Freudian Analysis and Research Library (CFAR) | Includes bibliographical references and index.
Identifiers: LCCN 2025016955 (print) | LCCN 2025016956 (ebook) | ISBN 9781032637525 hardback | ISBN 9781032637501 paperback | ISBN 9781032637549 ebook
Subjects: LCSH: Lacan, Jacques, 1901–1981 | Jealousy | Psychoanalysis
Classification: LCC BF575.F4 L33 2026 (print) | LCC BF575.F4 (ebook) | DDC 152.4/8—dc23/eng/20250724
LC record available at https://lccn.loc.gov/2025016955
LC ebook record available at https://lccn.loc.gov/2025016956

ISBN: 978-1-032-63752-5 (hbk)
ISBN: 978-1-032-63750-1 (pbk)
ISBN: 978-1-032-63754-9 (ebk)

DOI: 10.4324/9781032637549

Typeset in Times New Roman
by Apex CoVantage, LLC

Contents

Contributors' bios

Anouchka Grose is a psychoanalyst and writer. Her published books include: *From Anxiety to Zoolander: Notes on Psychoanalysis* (Karnac, 2018), *A Guide to Eco-Anxiety: How to Protect the Planet and Your Mental Health* (Watkins, 2020), *Uneasy Listening: Notes on Hearing and Being Heard* (Mack, 2022), and *Fashion: A Manifesto* (Notting Hill Editions, 2023). She also writes about art and fashion, and has contributed to *The Guardian, Granta, Harper's Bazaar*, and Radio 4.

Darian Leader is a psychoanalyst and author. He is a founding member of the Centre for Freudian Analysis and Research (CFAR) in London. His books include *The New Black: Mourning, Melancholia and Depression* (2008), *What Is Madness?* (2011); *Strictly Bipolar* (2013); *Why Can't We Sleep?* (2019); *Jouissance: Sexuality, Suffering, and Satisfaction* (2021); and *Is It Ever Just Sex?* (2023). He writes frequently about contemporary art.

Geneviève Morel is a psychoanalyst practicing in Paris and Lille. A graduate of the École Normale Supérieure, she holds an agrégation in mathematics and a doctorate in psychology. She is a founding member of CP-ALEPH, editor-in-chief of the journal *Savoirs et clinique*, and a member of CFAR. She is the author of several books, including *Tueuses* (érès, 2024), *Terroristes* (Fayard, 2018), *The Law of the Mother* (Routledge, 2019), and *Sexual Ambiguities* (Karnak, 2011).

Renata Salecl is a philosopher and sociologist. She is Professor of Psychology and Psychoanalysis of Law at the School of Law, Birkbeck College, University of London, and a Senior Researcher at the Institute of Criminology at the Faculty of Law in Ljubljana, Slovenia. Her books, which have been translated into 20 languages, include *A Passion for Ignorance: What We Choose Not to Know and Why* (Princeton UP, 2020), *Tyranny of Choice* (Profile Books, 2011), *On Anxiety* (Routledge, 2004), and *(Per)versions of Love and Hate* (Verso, 1998). Renata's work has been presented at TED Global. In addition to her scholarly work, she has published catalogue essays on artists Francis Bacon, Jenny Holzer, Anthony Gormley, and Sarah Sze. She is also active in the civil initiative "Airspace Tribunal," which is engaged in the initiative to propose a new human right to protect the freedom to live without physical or psychological threats from above.

Akshi Singh is a writer working across poetry, memoir, and fiction, and a Lacanian psychoanalyst in formation. Her first book, *In Defence of Leisure* (Vintage Books, 2025), describes reading the work of the modernist writer, psychoanalyst, and painter Marion Milner. She is an associate editor at *Parapraxis* magazine, and deputy editor at *Critical Quarterly.* Her writing has appeared in *Art Monthly, Texte zur Kunst, The London Review of Books*, and *Parapraxis* magazine.

Kristina Valendinova is a psychoanalyst living and working in London, and a member of CFAR and the Cercle Freudien in Paris. She is the cofounder of Bubble and Speak, a maison-verte style drop-in for parents and small children in London.

Jamieson Webster is a psychoanalyst in New York City, part-time faculty at The New School for Social Research, and faculty and board member of Pulsion International Institute. She is the author of *Disorganisation and Sex* (Divided, 2022) and *On Breathing* (Peninsula, 2025).

Carmen Wright is a psychoanalyst, writer, and member of the Centre for Freudian Analysis and Research, where she sometimes teaches. She also works with infants and carers at Bubble and Speak, a Françoise Dolto–inspired Maison Verte. She is based in London.

Acknowledgements

Thank you to Anouchka Grose for inviting me to submit something, for her show of enthusiasm when I did, and for her kindness throughout my training – I would not have made it through without you. A heartfelt thanks to all the contributors for responding to the project with such gusto, and for making the subject your own. To Darian Leader, thank you for quietly supporting me to get my words out, in ways both known and unknown to me. I have immense gratitude to the students, trainees, and members of CFAR that have attended any talks I have given – your engagement in what I have had to say has been a huge encouragement. Thanks to my supervisors and teachers at CFAR, especially Astrid Gessert, who has been a constant beacon. Thank you to Gabriella Boyd for allowing me to use her wonderful painting, *Sunhead* (2017), for the cover. Thanks to the friends who have borne my jealousy and my thoughts on jealousy, and who offered thought-provoking comments in response: Martha Barratt, Rose Eagle-Hull, Yannick Hill, Daniel Mapp, Matthew McGough, Hanna Schaefer, Natasha Silver, Akshi Singh, Georgia Tomlinson, Miriam Tobin, and Kristina Valendinova – especially to Martha and Miriam, for their careful and generous close readings. Thank you to my patients, past and present, for teaching me about being human. Finally thank you always to JR, for everything.

Chapter 1

Introduction

Carmen Wright

The first friend I ever made was a twin. One of my earliest memories is of the three of us going to the paddling pool, age three or so. When we ran back to our parents nearby squealing with delight and dripping from head to toe, I remember the two of them being wrapped up by a single towel, which gathered their shivering bodies together, snug. I was offered my own separate towel, which suddenly appeared sad, deficient. The feeling was instant: total abandonment, hatred of their union, despair, desperate attempts to be a part of what could not include me, bewilderment and disgust written on their faces.

It is interesting to me now that I chose to befriend a twin, as though my three-year-old curiosity was drawn precisely, tragically, to instances of my own exclusion. A girlhood of attempts to obtain a Best Friend, or invite frenzied breakdowns of who-likes-who-best, furthered and fed this curiosity of mine. But what was being aimed at here? We could guess it was an attempt to learn more about whatever I was excluded *from*, in some unlikely bid at its prevention, but this is where jealousy starts to eat itself: what can it possibly mean to gain knowledge of that which excludes you, of that which, by definition, you cannot know?

This pursuit mercifully toned down with age, yet I still see a parallel between these early episodes of jealousy and the uncloseable gap that exists between people, the impossibility of grasping anyone's inner life for oneself, or in totality – or, as one tweet put it: 'some ppl [*sic*] really ruin their lives trying to experience third person feelings in the first person'.[1] Not surprisingly, this shows up on a daily basis in the contemporary psychoanalytic clinic. Almost every patient speaks at some point to the tragic combination of confusion, yearning, and betrayal that comes from reckoning with exclusion, often hiding behind more palatable expressions of 'feeling unwanted', which tends to fix the problem to specific occurrences, or to others' failures to fulfil a duty of care. It can also show up in a totally defended form, as in accusation – 'they *never* loved me!' – but when unpacked carefully, there is often something being articulated that is harder to endure than simple rejection, far less ego-syntonic, about desire's ebb and flow. For all that, what I have learned through editing this collection, trying myself to write about and understand jealousy, is that there can be no end to this lesson – no moment of acceptance which

DOI: 10.4324/9781032637549-1

finally kills the feeling dead. Jealousy laughs in the face of enlightenment: a thirst for knowledge plays right into its hand.

Despite any final conversion of our jealousy now seeming decidedly hopeless, the idea for this collection began with the question of whether we have, to the contrary, successfully diminished its importance in our social relationships. For a great effort has been made in contemporary Western culture to renegotiate old prohibitions, to reorganise our sex lives, relationships, and family structures in new and inventive ways – ways which appear to involve less and less renunciation. Could this be a sign we are less bothered by jealousy, or only that we long to be? There is certainly a general confidence in its irrelevance; we even have a new word, 'compersion', to describe how *not* jealous we are, meaning 'positive feelings about your partner's other intimacies'.[2] And there seems no end to articles arguing that open relationships are better suited to our much longer lives, or that the nuclear family will have to go when the resources run out, that we'll have to finally learn to share. There is only the minor problem of jealousy, which is no real problem at all: 'if you feel attractive and loved, if you believe your partner won't leave you, and if you start to think differently about society's insistence on monogamy, jealousy becomes less relevant' as one writer puts it (Werber, 2024).

Behind this now widespread idea that non-monogamy is more socially progressive, though, is a clinical question receiving very little attention: what *is* jealousy? Is it, as the author of the previous quote supposes, a response to feeling unattractive or unloved, or believing you will be left? Or is this a red herring – the conscious concerns voiced by the jealous, but a far cry from a description of how the feeling functions psychically, or what might explain its presence, absence, or intensity? The supposition that it should be easy to dismiss (meaning, usually, the partner should just provide greater reassurance) is hard on everyone involved and appears to be leading to a lot of shame: many report feeling like a failure (or worse, like a heteronormative bore) if they notice hurt feelings when partners stray away, or a desire to 'close off' a relationship. In any case, the psychoanalytic literature suggests the matter is more complex than this easy dismissal would have us believe – perhaps, even, to a dizzying degree.

Freud on jealousy

Outside of his paper 'Some Neurotic Mechanisms in Jealousy, Paranoia and Homosexuality', published relatively late in his analytic career in 1922, Freud made little attempt to offer a definition of jealousy, even though the feeling could be said to reach right to the heart of the psychoanalytic project. Nonetheless, he uses the term plentifully, as when he speaks of delusional jealousy in the Schreber case in 1911 as a means of illustrating paranoia; when he states cursorily in the 'Three Essays on the Theory of Sexuality' in 1905 that 'Jealousy in a lover is never without an infantile root or at least an infantile reinforcement' (1905a, p. 228); or when he highlights its foundational significance to identification in Group Psychology (p. 105). Mostly, his writings appeal to jealousy as a lever to enter other ideas. This is instructive of the way the feeling has tendrils reaching into an abundance of psychological phenomena, as also evidenced by the diverse range of theories of jealousy in the literature. It has been linked to love, to oedipal and sibling complexes, to oral fixation; and has been conceived as a defence against guilt, or shame, or penis or womb envy, or as having a hand in furthering identification and social feeling, to name a few. The 1922 paper itself examines jealousy only in the first three pages – but as is often the case with Freud, this was enough space to offer numerous starting points which later psychoanalysts have pursued.

Jealousy, he observes, is a normal part of human experience and is

> essentially compounded of grief, the pain caused by the thought of losing the loved object, and of the narcissistic wound, in so far as this is distinguishable from the other wound; further, of feelings of enmity against the successful rival, and of a greater or lesser amount of self-criticism which tries to hold the subject's own ego accountable for his loss.
>
> (1922, p. 223)

Nevertheless, Freud thought jealousy has varying 'grades'. 'Normal or competitive' jealousy is 'a continuation of the earliest stirrings of the child's affective life, [which] originates in the Oedipus or brother-and-sister complex' (1922, p. 223). It is the echo and persistence of feelings that arise from learning we are not the sole priority of those we depend on, usually awoken by the worry or experience of being usurped by a sibling or parent. This is something which, *if* encountered – and there are many who do not experience such a 'fall' – is never satisfactorily managed, always involves loss and disappointment at a minimum, hence the tendency for its 'continuation' and its normalcy.

Projected jealousy, by contrast, works not to continue to express but to keep the subject's own inclinations towards infidelity *unexpressed*. Inclinations which Freud refreshingly acknowledges to be par for the course in any relationship:

> Anyone who denies these temptations in himself will nevertheless feel their pressure so strongly that he will be glad enough to make use of an unconscious mechanism to alleviate his situation. He can obtain this alleviation – and, indeed, acquittal by his conscience – if he projects his own impulses to faithlessness on to the partner to whom he owes faith. This strong motive can then make use of the perceptual material which betrays unconscious impulses of the same kind in the partner.
>
> (p. 224)

What makes projected jealousy so fiddly is that the person is usually on to something about their partner's unconscious – but their feeling of righteousness comes not from this, but from their own knowledge of the unconscious, which they project. A better solution to our desirous natures, and one which social convention[3] has allowed for, is to agree to a 'safety valve' – a degree of 'latitude' when it comes to flirtations – which safeguard against actual infidelity, with the benefit of reverting released desires back towards the partner (p. 224). But both members of the couple must agree to not go sniffing around in their partner's unconscious. There are some for whom this is intolerable, and it is in this population that projected jealousy operates, serving to keep knowledge of such desires in abeyance.

Delusional jealousy is also presented by Freud as a defence which operates to keep the person's own inclinations out of consciousness, but this time it's a homosexual desire which has been foreclosed, unregistered even unconsciously, meaning the jealous conviction thus arrives with unshakable certainty: '*I* do not love him, *she* loves him' (p. 225). Freud characteristically spends the remainder of the paper then casting doubt on this explanation, suggesting homosexuality may also proceed from jealous feeling, not only the other way around. Whatever we want to say of this theory, it leaves Freud somewhat undecided on how jealousy becomes in some cases so insurmountable.

The post-Freudians

Post-Freudian psychoanalytic literature on jealousy has mostly developed the ways in which it functions dynamically, to keep confronting ideas out of consciousness, but there has been much deliberation over what such ideas consist of. Hotly contested was whether jealousy originates in, and thus defends against, oedipal *or* pre-oedipal preoccupations. To give a taste of some of the influential theories, I'll focus on Ernest Jones, Joan Riviere, and Otto Fenichel, each of whose work on the subject tries to get to the bottom of it.

After Freud's 1922 paper, Ernest Jones gave a lecture at the Sorbonne in Paris in 1929, published in the *Revue Française de Psychanalyse* in the same year. He agrees with Freud that jealousy's routes lie in the Oedipus complex, but he emphasises the *second* wound mentioned by Freud, the wound to the subject's narcissism. 'More secret, but probably more important . . . is the wound experienced by the lover in his *self-esteem*, in what psychoanalysis calls narcissism', Jones writes (p. 232, my translation). Contrary to the cultural characterisation of jealousy as a marker of passionate love, Jones thought that the jealous person is in fact *incapable* of loving actively, since their trouble with self-esteem leads them to crave to be loved instead of to love. Which is to say he reverses Freud's idea: it's not that jealousy produces a wound to narcissism, but that a wounded narcissism, what he refers to as a 'feeling of inferiority', produces jealousy (p. 237). Thus, jealousy is for Jones an expression of a demand to be loved as a way of making up for a self-love that is missing. But it is a faulty mechanism, for the demand to be loved short-circuits the act of loving, such that the jealous subject remains stuck in this passive position.

Jones then argues that because 'in the final analysis any feeling of inferiority, whether mental or physical, has as its starting point a feeling of *moral* inferiority, a feeling of *guilt*', it is therefore unconscious *guilt* from oedipal situations that lies behind the jealous person's wounded self-esteem (p. 237). Jealousy emerges, then, not only as an outcome of low self-esteem which is founded on unconscious guilt, but also as a means of *treating* that guilt, as it were, since in jealousy, one 'exaggerate[s] the criminality of others and violently put[s] the right to [one's] own side' (p. 239). Jones's argument then gets rather convoluted. In the jealous person, he thinks, Oedipal guilt leads to an 'excessive *dependence* on the object loved', and through this there emerges, as Riviere paraphrases, a 'fear of inversion and of the father', with the 'inversion lead[ing] to fear of the woman, from which flight and infidelity arises', and it is this 'infidelity' which is finally projected onto the partner in jealousy ('Jealousy as a Mechanism of Defence', 1932, p. 415).

Three years later in 1932, Joan Riviere offers up a pre-oedipal case of jealousy that she suggests may have some 'general validity'. Riviere expands on Jones's idea of jealousy as a defence against unconscious guilt, but this time guilt bound up with oral-sadistic urges. She thought Freud's idea that projected jealousy indicates a repressed inclination towards infidelity was merely a superficial account, and she presents a case where the *appearance* of such a projection was used by her patient as a defence against *another* function of the jealousy: as a projection of a dominant unconscious fantasy situation. This unconscious fantasy 'consisted of an impulse or an act on the patient's part of seizing and obtaining from some other person something she greatly desired, thus robbing and despoiling him or her' (p. 416). It was the fulfilment of this unconscious fantasy that could be said to be 'the ruling passion of her life': her pleasure was always acquired *at someone else's expense* (pp. 416–417). To illustrate this, Riviere includes the patient's conscious masturbation fantasy, that of *a young girl in a doctor's consulting room, being undressed and then examined by him; there is another woman in the background* (p. 419). In Riviere's reading, her patient is gaining satisfaction from the idea of 'robbing the other woman of [the doctor], outraging and despoiling her', whilst at the same time 'the doctor's sadistic stripping of the girl was a reversal of him as her agent robbing the woman to give all to the girl' (p. 419).

Apart from reporting this masturbation fantasy, Riviere does not offer up all the details of the case, so we must take her word for it when she says, 'the origin of the phantasy [is] in the oral-erotic and oral-sadistic phase of development' (p. 420). It is these oral-sadistic urges which the subject attributes, via projected jealousy, to the other, by whom the subject begins to feel threatened. What jealousy defends *against* is thus anxiety and guilt produced by the subject's own sadism, now conceived as coming from the other. This sadism arises out of oral envy during weaning, and a feeling of having been deprived of the breast which is now given to the other. You can see here how her paper also paves the way for Klein's later work, *Envy and Gratitude* in 1957. Jealousy, Riviere thinks, harks back to this oral phase of development rather than merely to triangular situations involving *object*-love – for Riviere, it is part-objects (the breast, the penis) that the infant feels deprived of. Her point is that just because the unconscious fantasy appears to involve three agents, this does not mean that it involves object-love. Her patient's jealousy was never *rooted* in a triangular situation, she thought; rather, a triangular situation was beckoned in as a means of working through an oral preoccupation.

So, it is the feeling of envious deprivation that Riviere thinks lies behind the demand for love exhibited by the jealous. Her theory helps to explain why the subject thus cannot be convinced of the love which they demand, since unbeknownst to them it is something 'deeper' than the genital relation to a parent that they demand, and the deeper sense of deprivation which they suffer from cannot therefore be alleviated by promises in object-love. We could link Riviere's ideas to Ernest Jones here: remember that he thought the jealous person *incapable of love*, that is to say, *object-love* (which he calls 'genital love'). Jones likewise locates a propensity towards jealousy logically prior to properly 'genital' forms of loving others: the jealousy is rooted more in the narcissistic, passive aim of being loved than in the later phase of properly genital love – except Jones does not follow this through by locating jealousy prior to the Oedipus complex.

Otto Fenichel adds to this complex picture of jealousy's defensive function in his 1953 paper 'A Contribution to the Psychology of Jealousy'. He makes the point that if jealousy were a mere matter of the *expression* of the subject's hatred towards a frustrating object combined with envy towards an other that is more gratified than oneself, then we would expect firstly that the object frustrating the subject be *loved* – when, as Jones showed, there is a greater emphasis on *being loved* than on *loving actively* in jealousy – and secondly, we would expect that jealousy would *therefore*, like all other unpleasurable reactions to a frustration, undergo *repression*. But the opposite is the case with jealousy – it is entirely obtrusive and often becomes what Fenichel calls a 'supervalent idea' (1953, p. 361). Thus, he thought that, like all other supervalent ideas, jealousy 'must serve to repress something *else*, it must – as all screen memories do – bring the jealous person a certain advantage in the economy of his libido' (p. 362).

Fenichel falls somewhere between the Jonesian model and Riviere's account. He agrees with Jones that the jealous person is someone for whom a loss of love is a greater narcissistic injury than most, since *to be* loved is more important for them than loving, which implies they have not attained 'genital primacy' (p. 362). Fenichel puts this very succinctly: in intensely jealous people, 'narcissistic and erotic needs are insufficiently differentiated from each other', adding that these needs tend to become blurred when we are in love anyway, hence why all people in love are inclined to become jealous (p. 362). He then adds to this Riviere's observations, arguing that jealousy is chronic when this narcissistic dependency on the loved object coincides with an oral fixation. Orally fixated people, he thought, rely upon the external world more or less exclusively for the regulation of their self-regard. He describes a jealous woman patient of his, for whom the analyst's words and friendliness meant an 'oral supply from without', which was important to the patient to 'maintain' her self-regard – if he failed in this task now and then, she would console herself by eating a cake from the pastry shop (p. 366).

But both Jones's and Fenichel's theories paint the jealous person as a fantasist, a drain on well-adapted individuals who love themselves properly and who can therefore find satisfying 'genital' relations in love – Jones even uses the term 'incomplete' to describe the jealous subject (1929, p. 236). Fenichel thinks the jealous subject needs to learn how to differentiate between their erotic and narcissistic needs – as though a person's self-esteem can and should be fully siphoned off from the tendency to ask for or be shown love by others. Yet even in Freud's cursory description of jealousy, he underlines that this is not so easy to do – remember his comment about it not always being possible to distinguish between the first wound of losing the loved object from the second, narcissistic wound, i.e. of what that says about *you*. Which is to say, Jones and Fenichel succumb to a notion of the object that could satisfy the subject, leaving them with stable, harmonious boundaries. In a Lacanian landscape, where no such harmony is possible, where there is an intractable dissatisfaction to the subject-object relationship, where in fact it is those that theorise completion who are the fantasists – in that world, couldn't we say the jealous person is very forthright in pointing this out? 'I am not enough for you!' they proclaim, again and again. And aren't they right?[4]

Lacan on jealousy

In Lacan's earlier work, jealousy is likewise figured as executing a psychic function, but instead of appealing to the concept of defence (which begs this seemingly interminable question: against what?), he highlights its binding capacity. Jealousy is a primal mode of identification, he suggests, necessary for our first entrance into the social world. His comments in *Family Complexes* (1938) neutralise some of the confusion around jealousy's pre- versus post-oedipal origin by introducing a sequence to Freud's original idea: the sibling complex – what Lacan calls 'the intrusion complex' in this paper – precedes the Oedipus complex, and it is with the intrusion complex that jealousy emerges properly for the first time, and which the later Oedipus complex is founded on and works over. At a certain moment in the infant's life, they come to encounter the fact that they are not the only one, that they lack something which the other has, giving rise to jealousy.

Lacan goes on to argue that the subject's identification with another child at the core of jealousy provides a solution to the problem thrown up by the previous stage of the 'Weaning Complex', that of sublimating the maternal imago, and the death wish that this gives rise to. Jealousy solves this by *creating* an object in the form of a rival. Kristina Valendinova will offer us a detailed account of this theory in Chapter 7. Through identifying with this rival, the subject also achieves a split in the self, helping to distance them from their primary masochism. A gap is opened up, and two become three – or, more accurately, the third activates the fact that there were two, not one.

In other words, jealousy is the first point at which human culture *interprets* the facts of nature, offering it a gloss; not, as Lacan characterises Riviere's thesis, simply an outcome of these facts of nature (the scarcity of resources). The gloss jealousy creates is twofold: the third is both rival and (as an immediate consequence of which) friend. But because there remains some confusion between identification and love in the imaginary identification with the rival in jealousy, which will only be differentiated and stabilised (if at all) by the later Oedipus complex, Oedipus likewise has a hand in furthering a heretofore rudimentary form of jealousy. In other words, with the oedipal triangle comes the dawning of desire's direction of travel, which gives the losses involved in jealousy, so aptly described by Freud, their stakes.

This is an interesting idea, because as well as settling the confusion about jealousy's origin (now oedipal yet only because also pre-oedipal, which is to say it's not the developmental phase that matters so much as the dialectical relation between the two), it would also help explain the oft-commented-upon absence of object-love in jealousy. Rather than pathologising its absence, as Jones and Fenichel do,[5] Lacan points out that jealousy is a socially beneficial form of identification which *gives way* to loving, rather than being predicated on it (as in classical oedipal identification).

It was of course Freud who originally highlighted the existence of a mode of identification that supersedes object-love in 'Group Psychology'[6] – though not until *after* he had spent some years assuming priority to a libidinal link, as we saw in his erroneous interpretation of who Dora was interested in (1905b). The later Freud offers the example of

> the troop of women and girls, all of them in love in an enthusiastically sentimental way, who crowd round a singer after his performance. It would certainly be easy for each of them to be jealous of the rest; but, in the face of their numbers and the consequent impossibility of their reaching the aim of their love, they renounce it.
>
> (1921, p. 107)

Which is to say, it is *jealousy* that instigates this mode of identifying, which does not have object-love as its aim, and which instead leads to positive social feeling. As Freud notes at the end of 'Some Neurotic Mechanisms': 'the birth of the social instincts in the individual' arise out of 'jealous or hostile impulses which cannot achieve satisfaction' (1922, pp. 231–232).

In *Family Complexes*, Lacan reinvigorates Freud's point, bringing home, in a characteristically dramatic fashion, its final consequence: jealousy has a role 'in the genesis of sociability and, through that, of human consciousness itself' (1938, p. 16). Jealousy cleverly redirects the very pain of exclusion that it is founded on to achieve sociability as an end in itself. An end which, we might say, has happier results than the longed-for imagined relationship: the 'group swooning' that Freud's women partake in affords them greater togetherness than a fantasised love-relation to the admired man (upon which that jealous identification is made possible) could hope to offer.

Introduction to the chapters

This mutual dependence of jealousy and identification is one amongst a few themes which recur in the chapters that follow. In Chapter 9, I link Lacan's comments on this to D.W. Winnicott's perspective: both associate identification beckoned by jealousy at an early age to the ability to grapple with the real feelings of others for the first time. I ask whether, if it's true that jealousy really is less prolific today, this suggests we are turning away from the realness of others, showing an intolerance to the disillusionment that realness must confer on us, and perhaps becoming *less* relational, in the process. Which is to say, whether jealousy might be good for something after all.

In Chapter 4, Geneviève Morel shows us the ways the mutual dependence of identification and jealousy can morph into something dangerous. She identifies this in *invidia*, sometimes translated as jealousy and sometimes envy, highlighting the way such a distinction becomes obsolete when the experience intensifies, and 'a feeling of extreme and unique bitterness' descends. She explains that 'what is characteristic of *invidia* is precisely this commingling of love and identification, which engenders aggressivity as a consequence'. If love and identification do not come untethered, then aggression has no outlet.

Morel's chapter unpacks Lacan's subtle shift in emphasis when it comes to psychotic jealousy. Where for Freud, negation and projection is the last word on the matter, for Lacan there is a direct link between 'the violence of aggressiveness and psychotic negation: the foreclosed refusal to recognise one's own fascination with the rival is what drives the jealous person to the very extremes'. The case of Lucie highlights the way that maintaining such negation can make a subject liable to violence. It was her 'foreclosed fixation on her rival' that was 'the seed of the uncontrollable violence that will be triggered later, in any situation of rivalry or betrayal', a violence which repeats throughout Lucie's life and culminates in her stabbing a man *50 times* ('just think of the rage [this] takes'). Morel reminds us that despite jealousy's kindling of identification in Lacan's intrusion complex, if the Oedipus complex cannot sufficiently disperse that jealousy by localising identification, *invidia* may lay in wait.

Yet, as Darian Leader points out in Chapter 3, we can also see the apparent success of an oedipal cure, albeit structurally tempering matters, *aggravating* jealous feeling. He suggests that understanding the different meaning of possession and ownership can shed light on this puzzling clinical phenomenon, when linked to what Lacan emphasised through his reading of Oedipus: not only the registration of maternal absence, but the second question of whether the signification of loss has been *inscribed*. Such an inscription achieves a tempering nodal point without a concrete fixity: its malleability is both strength and weakness, the weakness being inevitable flare-ups of jealous feeling – 'however normative the passage through the Oedipus and castration complex might be, jealousy remains as a residue and a potential due precisely to [the] non-ownership at the heart of ownership', Leader writes. He highlights two popular readings of jealousy – either it can function to negate desire, where the interest is generally located properly with the rival; or it can function to highlight the incongruence between phallic and non-phallic sexuality. In the former, possession and ownership are soldered together; in the latter, they are broken apart.

At the same time, Leader's chapter highlights that *without* the inscription of a third-party function, jealousy may likewise be called in to provide an answer to the dreadful question of maternal desire left open. Not to mention its working over of an archaic oral envy, decipherable in the example of groups of adolescent girls intent on the prising away of one girl from another, seemingly operating in the service not of personal gain but at the Other's loss. Which is all to say the registration of the mother's absences and the later oedipal dimension of having, not having, and gifts ought not to be confused, Leader reminds us, and their many combinations can help explain the variety of responses in jealousy, where say one's jealous rage can be both tamed and aggravated by the right combination. As Freud highlighted then, Leader reaffirms the way jealousy is not reducible to one form, even though the feeling is still unmistakable – better to refer to *jealousies* in the clinic.

Connected, perhaps, to this apparent ubiquity, writers have also highlighted jealousy's insuperability: the way it 'can only be alleviated and tolerated, it can't be done away with', as Akshi Singh notes in Chapter 6. As Jamieson Webster also does in Chapter 8, Singh points to the way jealousy is both symptom of and treatment for any experience that resonates with the 'shock and incomprehension of the primal scene', our first proper experience of exclusion. Like a Freudian compulsion to repeat, then, jealousy circles that same painful wound, repetitively, not quite managing to do something new with that early trauma. Singh carries us into the subjective crevices of what it is like to feel this, to be rudely confronted with our lack, our incapacity to wholly captivate the other, yet also how this offers a freedom and an entrance into writerly expression that couldn't do without this. Seeking points of our exclusion here is not only a pain but the (only?) position from which we might *say* something that isn't merely for the sake of that attempted captivation – be it via rhetorical persuasion, touting of the university discourse, etc. In Chapter 6, she asks,

> is there something about writing that allows it to occupy the same space as the lack that makes jealousy both inevitable and intolerable, so that relating to the world through writing necessarily means encountering the world, first and foremost, through a lack that can't be overcome?

The question of jealousy's interaction with the social realm is taken up in many of the chapters. Because the feeling can lead to loving *and* hateful behaviour, it leaves a lot of room for variety, as Anouchka Grose argues in Chapter 2:

> you might hate the person who appears to be trying to dislodge you with regard to the one you love. Or you might hate your lover for their apparent disloyalty. With envy, you may seek to destroy the person who appears to have what you lack, or you may decide to align yourself with them, making of them an ego ideal.

In a strict sense, then, it is impossible to say with any reliability whether jealousy is a help or a hindrance to the social – only that it involves both hate and love, and the person needs to do something with both. In Chapter 9 I revisit this debate: all things considered, is jealousy on the side of the good or the bad? And why, indeed, does it so often come down to a debate over ethics when we discuss the subject?

Grose notes the fact that jealousy and envy 'erupt with regard to *having* or *not having*' means these feelings also influence and are influenced by economic systems, and the ideologies and cultures that develop from them. Jealousy and envy are encouraged in socioeconomic systems in which property and ownership is foregrounded, which stand to benefit from our striving to have more and a pouting about having-not. This begs the question as to whether, without a culture that is obsessed with possessing, we would really be all that jealous and envious? Even if we want to say this overplays the influence of socioeconomic systems on the origin of feelings, Grose highlights the value of thinking about what might happen to socioeconomic systems if we try to deal with our jealousy and envy differently – if we face it, talk through it, and crucially do not avoid acting in ways that provoke it.

She takes us into the fascinating world of Tamera for a radical alternative, a community which seeks not to deny jealous feelings yet also one that refuses to organise social relations around them. Grose makes the illuminating suggestion that a collective identification with some greater purpose could be important to bear such feelings – in Tamera's case, it's the fight against fascism. Importantly here, though, free love is not placed in opposition to monogamy; rather, Tamera members are encouraged to love however they choose, and 'monogamy and asexuality are also considered perfectly acceptable options'. This is quite different to 'the emotional hellscape known as urban polyamory, with its rules, rotas and sickening cocktail of fomo, competition, and acquisitiveness, not to mention the likely involvement of an app' – and, these days, quite a bit of pressure *not* to cave in to monogamy.

In Chapter 5, Salecl links what Grose notices about the culturally contingent treatment of jealousy to its social function: 'jealousy is a necessary mark of socialisation, which is why the way we deal with jealousy, how we express it or suppress it, is very much marked by culture'. But she also highlights that it goes both ways: 'jealousy is also exploited by ideology', as we see with consumerism, racism, sexism, and so on, where the perceived enjoyment of others motivates (and is used to justify) violence, as well as operating as a decoy for positive forms of social change. She illustrates the way jealousy can be powerfully evoked in relation to a social role, when somebody else may have received an apparently superior one. Which is to say, the way both jealousy and envy serve to constantly track the symbolic realm, the realm of who we are for others, in what way we are recognised, something Leader noticed becomes pivotal at a certain point for teenage girls. Yet this tracking function can often be pacifying; we focus intently on the better fortunes of others, preventing us from seeing 'the broader picture of the system in which [we] live'.

Nonetheless, this symbolic tracking shows an investment in the social realm, something which, many of the contributors point out, requires jealousy to be instilled in the first place. As Kristina Valendinova writes, jealousy and envy are 'not merely personal afflictions but fundamental mechanisms in the genesis of social and psychic structures'. To Grose's question as to whether these feelings would be as pervasive without being so socioeconomically convenient,

Valendinova suggests it could be the other way around, that such feelings have a hand in the formation of our socioeconomic environments. Valendinova helpfully unpacks Lacan's dense argument in *Family Complexes*, linking these ideas to contemporary clinical examples.

Sometimes, jealous feelings travel so far from their presupposed location in the psychic as to become unrecognisable; but look a little closer, and plenty of social issues could be said to contain the hallmarks of jealousy. In Chapter 8, Jamieson Webster shows us with a terrifying momentum the layers of connection between the far right, America's historic suppression of mothers, and a sense of jealous entitlement to the mother's attention, not to say self-sacrifice. It is not mere coincidence, she argues, that the violent attacks on women's rights in the United States in recent years have centred on a woman's right over her womb, over her ability to procreate. Behind them, we can detect a possessiveness over the mother's body, a demand – via identification with the would-be aborted infant – to be the *only one*, meaning she renounce whatever else is taking up her attention and return it exclusively to her unborn child. Here, then, in an inversion of Riviere's account, it is jealousy which precedes envy, and envy which enacts something of jealousy's aim. Webster observes that the ubiquity of the gaze, made manifest by our contemporary penchant for images, is a sign of that jealousy. The 'everywhere' gaze – the notion of there being some higher order of enjoyment which the subject won't ever reach, and about which they can know nothing (except whatever they can glean from an image), yet it's a point they judge themselves from – works, then, to support and entrench our jealous entitlement and disappointment.

Writing on so-called womb or birth envy is well developed in writing by Kleinian psychoanalysts even though it tends to be, in Léon Wurmser's words, 'undervalued, even omitted, in favour of "penis envy"' in the psychoanalytic theory on jealousy (2008, p. xiii). Leader notes the hesitancy of stressing the relevance of envy to jealousy in the Lacanian field because of its association to womb and mother envy, which are 'ridiculed in our milieu. Better just to say the phallic function needs to appropriate the not-all'. Yet time and again, we find the envying of pregnancy, of procreation and associations to all things maternal have an outsize influence on jealousy, a theme shown in Webster's as well as Morel's chapter.

The *invidia* in the case of Morel's Lucie returns to that same envy: 'in her murderous attacks against her love-objects, wasn't she ultimately trying to kill this original mother, one who had been loved but was a bad mother?'. Morel clarifies that in feminine jealousy in particular, the phallic dimension is only superficial – penis envy, where it does feature, is not cause but symptom. What is far more significant is the perfect cocktail of hateloving, identification, aggression, and envy in relation to the realm of the maternal. She observes that it is often the 'inability to separate themselves from their mother, from the "maternal thing" devouring them from the inside' that is frequently found in female killers. Some forms of jealousy can function to support that inability, we might argue, for it forecloses separateness, reading the *I* as *you*.

It's funny in a way that jealousy, a feeling which so many of the contributors point out takes pride of place in psychoanalytic theory ('The various machinations of the Oedipus complex offer us a matrix of jealousies and envies that ultimately form our characters', writes Grose in Chapter 2), returns so pointedly to that which most people use and need psychoanalysis for: to talk about our mothers, or, more accurately, about our disappointment in relation to them. There is a lesson here about what happens when we don't reflect upon this disappointment, when an honest look at our drives, desires, and fantasies is missed – for Webster, it leads to a violent misogyny and a barely concealed attempt to control and master women's bodies.

Conclusion

Is the lesson here that jealousy is better off embraced, acknowledged, *gone through*? By the same token, should we give up on our attempts at its transformation? Isn't this the formula espoused by Tamera: that a successful and enduring life of free love involves *more* processing of our jealousy, *not less*, and certainly not a wishful assumption that a collective belief in sexual freedom is enough to magic the feeling away? For jealousy to not become problematic, that is, it must be given a place in the system.

Because, of course, I identify strongly and jealously with the writers I asked to contribute – or perhaps because jealousy shares certain key properties – you will notice some repetition in the chapters. I hope this mirroring of thought in different words might elicit, if not a final conception or solution to our jealousy, then perhaps a performance of its galvanising force for social engagement. The collection seeks to take the temperature of jealousy today; what has changed about it, and where can it be located? Authors note the paradox that its social origin renders jealousy mouldable by a given culture in ways which determine how disruptive it can become to individual lives, yet also how, so long as we are social creatures, jealousy will invariably feature somewhere. Its chameleonic ability to attach itself to different areas of contemporary social life renders it no less alive, and certainly no less distinct.

Notes

1 Posted by 'no earthquake (world series baby)' and cited by Haley Nahman in '#187: Drowning in envy'. https://haleynahman.substack.com/p/187-drowning-in-envy, original tweet here. They follow it up with another: 'among other things through spectatorship or desire we project onto others idealised states of being that cannot be obtained as personal experiences'.
2 The word itself is not so new, but its population is recent. It was coined by the 'New Tribe' of the Kerista Commune in Haight-Ashbury, San Francisco (1971–1991). That configuration grew out of the 'Old Tribe' (1956–1970), a 1960s free-love movement with houses in New York, San Francisco, Los Angeles, and Berkeley and outposts in Belize and Roatan. See https://www.kerista.com/.

3 For Freud here, 'social convention' refers to the conventions of *his* society, without really acknowledging how much conventions can differ. Anouchka Grose asks in Chapter 2 about what effect such differences can have on how jealousy is dealt with.
4 Perhaps Freud too slips into a similar illusion, as Anne Dufourmantelle points out when she writes that 'whereas the mimetic conception of desire detaches it from any object, Freud clings to the idea of desire based on an object (the mother). Whereas the mimetic conception sees violence as a consequence of rivalry, Freud has to assume consciousness of the paternal rivalry and its deadly consequences' (2021, p. 78). She is contrasting Freud here not to Lacan, but to René Girard.
5 Jones locates a propensity towards jealousy logically prior to properly 'genital' forms of loving others: the jealousy is rooted more in the narcissistic, passive aim of being-loved than in the later phase of genital love. Fenichel likewise comments that the intensely jealous have not attained 'genital primacy', because their 'narcissistic and erotic needs are insufficiently differentiated from each other' (1953, p. 364).
6 Coincidentally – or perhaps not – the same year he wrote the jealousy paper, published a year later.

Reference list

Dufourmantelle, A. (2021). Jealousy. In *Defence of secrets* (L. Turner, Trans., pp. 77–78). Fordham University Press. (Original work published 2015).

Fenichel, O. (1953). A contribution to the psychology of jealousy. In H. Fenichel & D. Rapaport (Eds.), *The collected works of Otto Fenichel, first series*. W.W. Norton & Company.

Freud, S. (1905a). The three essays on the theory of sexuality. In *Standard edition* (Vol. 7, pp. 125–243). The Hogarth Press.

Freud, S. (1905b). Fragment of an analysis of a case of hysteria. In *Standard edition* (Vol. 7, pp. 3–122). The Hogarth Press.

Freud, S. (1921). Group psychology and the analysis of the ego. In *Standard edition* (Vol. 18, pp. 65–135). The Hogarth Press.

Freud, S. (1922). Some neurotic mechanisms in paranoia, jealousy and homosexuality. In *Standard edition* (Vol. 18, pp. 221–232). The Hogarth Press.

Jones, E. (1929). La Jalousie. *Revue Française de Psychanalyse*, *3*, 228–242.

Lacan, J. (1988). The family complexes. In C. Asp (Trans.), *Critical texts; a review of theory and criticism* (Vol. 5, Issue 3, pp. 12–29) (Original work published 1938).

Riviere, J. (1932). Jealousy as a mechanism of defence. *International Journal of Psychoanalysis*, *13*, 414–424.

Werber, C. (2024, April 20). My husband is my co-parent, friend and lover – but he isn't the only person I have sex with: the inside story of an open marriage. *The Guardian*. https://www.theguardian.com/lifeandstyle/2024/apr/20/open-marriage-cassie-werber#:~:text=If%20you%20feel%20attractive%20and,to%20be%20%E2%80%9Cnaturally%E2%80%9D%20jealous.

Wurmser, L., & Jarass, H. (2008). Jealousy and envy: New views about two powerful emotions. Routledge.

Chapter 2

Jealousy, monogamy, and utopian politics

Anouchka Grose

The place of jealousy in our emotional lives can be seen as a political matter. Is it a fundamental, unavoidable human emotion, like anger or sadness? Or do certain social conditions normalise and encourage possessiveness in love? For instance, in patrilineal societies where marriage laws support the passing of property from fathers to sons, the close policing of a wife's sexuality might be culturally sanctioned. Through a stroke of cunning, an existing emotional state becomes tied in with a social and legal framework, therefore ensuring the continuation of certain ways of life and economic practices. For Friedrich Engels in *The Origin of the Family, Private Property and the State* (1884), the insistence on the monogamous couple and their offspring as the economic unit of society was the source of widespread injustice and unhappiness, not to mention infidelity (which in itself was both a source and a result of injustice and unhappiness, particularly because the logic of marriage demanded 'monogamy *for the woman only*').

Other ways of life might encourage other emotional attitudes. For example, the indigenous activist and psychologist Geni Nuñez (2024) has spoken about the mutual confusion around the subject of what Christian missionaries and indigenous Brazilians believe constitutes a 'relationship'. While missionaries were busy trying to enforce the notion of a lifelong monogamous union between a man and a woman, they were sometimes disconcerted to find that the local word for 'partner' might equally be used to describe the loving relationship between friends and lovers, or between humans, trees, and rivers. This sometimes made it hard for them to work out, and therefore to control, who was doing what with whom. Having herself been trained as a missionary, Nuñez now campaigns to decolonise the sexual and sentimental practices of indigenous people.

The value given to jealousy has implications not only for people's love lives, but also for the ways in which they conceive of space, housing, family, and the future. In the first scenario, we see jealousy being used as an emotional support for wealth acquisition, inheritance, gender inequality, and private property. In the second, we don't. Hence the idea that non-monogamy can form part of a radical challenge to patriarchy and capitalism. But can people living in modern, industrialised societies simply decide to ditch certain behaviours and emotions in the name of politics, or does our emotional wiring get the better of us? In order to consider how one

DOI: 10.4324/9781032637549-2

might approach this question, we skip speedily through the history of monogamy in the Global North, take a brief look at jealousy as it appears in the psychoanalytic literature, consider a viral Tumblr post, and finally take as a case study a psycho-analytically informed intentional community who are researching alternatives to industrial modernity.

A brief history of monogamy

The standard UK civil wedding ceremony refers to the fact that marriage is for life, 'to the exclusion of all others'. If you break your vow, your spouse has the right to divorce you. The law supports monogamy, even if it doesn't actually enforce it. But why should it do that? What's supposedly in it for society?

People have tried to answer this question in so many different ways, it's dizzy-ing. There are evolutionary, economic, political, psychological, theological, his-torical, anthropological, and zoological explanations. To run quickly through some of the most popular theories:

First, you have evolutionary ideas such as that babies need more and longer care than other animals, therefore it helps if the parents form a lasting bond and bring the child up together. This is somewhat undermined by the fact that early human societies far from uniformly supported this family structure. Still, psychologically, there's the possibility that monogamy came to suit a lot of people thanks to human babies' need for so much close-up care. The necessary 'prematurity' of all human births, due to the massive head size of the infant, means that human parents and babies need to be strongly attached to one another; otherwise, babies would never survive. Because this early attachment is so vital to survival, it may make any threat to it extremely scary. The arrival of a new sibling might arouse a morbid fear; if your parents love *them*, will they also still love *you*? In this way, the promise of exclusivity in love might become extremely alluring in spite of all the problems it can bring. So, monogamy in adult life might signal a return to one's initial state of bound-up bliss. But what about the presence of the father? And possibly the grand-parents? And even friends and neighbours? Aren't most babies encouraged towards a certain kind of polyamory, a multitude of life-giving attachments?

If developmental theories can't quite explain the prevalence of monogamy in certain societies, you have the sociocultural idea that it arrives whenever a human group catches onto the idea of agriculture. Ploughing and sewing crops leads to private property, which in turn opens up the possibility of inheritance, meaning you need to know whose father you are, or aren't.

Because true sexual monogamy is so rare in nature – only 3 per cent of mam-mals do it – one imagines it might have been quite difficult for pioneering agricul-turalists to shrug off the sexual practices of their ancestors and to try something new and more restrictive. Over time, rules were developed so that only eldest sons could inherit. This meant you could practise non-monogamy if you wanted to, but your later progeny might find themselves second-class citizens after your death. Still, once you have agriculture, you also have a need for second-class citizens so everything could be argued to be progressing excellently, at least for the newly invented rich.

In the few hundred years BCE you get a jumble of ways of structuring romantic and sexual relationships. The Greeks and Romans were in favour of stay-at-home monogamous wives alongside far greater freedom for husbands, for whom visiting courtesans, seducing boys, and having sex with slaves were all options. However, there were various rules on how you went about it. If you were married, you weren't allowed to live with a lover, for instance.

All over Europe, Asia, the Middle East, China, and Latin America, we see a loose pattern of monogamy for the poor and polygyny for the rich. Still, there were often laws to protect wealthier women; in ancient Egypt, existing wives were allowed to divorce if they didn't like the set-up with their husbands' new spouses.

At the beginning of the Common Era, polygyny was still legal and practised all over Europe and the Middle East, in spite of the widespread myth of Adam and Eve and the notion of an exclusive, natural, heterosexual couple. There are plenty of multiple marriages in the *Five Books of Moses*, but only involving rich men. They also tend to get into terrible emotional trouble over it, like Abraham (who had quite a harrowing and complicated family life) and Jacob (who married a pair of sisters). The books also contain plenty of overt recommendations against multiple marriages and mention limits being placed on them, even for the rich. Plus they warn that first-born sons' rights have to be respected, even if the father no longer loves the mother. The New Testament is slightly more forthright on the subject of monogamy, making explicit reference to husbands and wives becoming one flesh, just as God intended. There's also the passage in Corinthians where Paul recommends, 'Because of the temptation to sexual immorality, each man should have his own wife and each woman her own husband'.

The Quran has a slightly different, but equally confusing, take. It says it's OK for a man to take up to four wives, but only on the condition that he is able to treat them all fairly. It then states that it's impossible to do this, and therefore one wife is the correct way forward. There's mention of acceptable concubinage, and also the fact that Muhammed had 11 female partners. But the law in the majority of Muslim countries now prohibits multiple marriages. Apparently, those passages in the Quran were applicable only at a particular point in history, when the devastation of war had led to a shortage of men.

Neither does the New Testament put a full blanket ban on polygamy. This idea was instituted later by politicians and lawmakers, who used particular interpretations of the Bible to manipulate the populace. They took little fragments, like the commandment not to covet thy neighbour's wife, and accentuated them. But why would anyone have an interest in this kind of social engineering? One theory, put forward by the American zoologist Richard Alexander in 1985, is that monogamous societies can manufacture bigger armies – an outcome much desired by Roman leaders. This is because across-the-board monogamy stops the big shots from monopolising the women, thereby making it easier for lower-status men to find wives. In order to make thousands of men risk their lives for you, you need to make sure you can offer them something they want. Apparently, men want women. So making women more widely available is a crowd-pleaser (a prototypical version of the incel dream). Having performed this incredible feat of magnanimity you then have to keep pumping out myths around love and marriage. This is because it turns out that, while men seem to want wives when there are no wives around, they also want to have sex with other women once they have wives (and of course, it works like that for the women too, but you had to keep quieter about this bit).

If history and religion don't persuade people that monogamy's a must, there's the fact that the much-studied prairie vole mates for life, which *surely* means we can too – apart from the fact that prairie voles are frequently sexually unfaithful, which is why they get so nasty with their neighbours during mating season. This also goes for swans, orangutans, and all manner of creatures previously idealised for their faithful ways.

Jealousy begins at home

In the most sweeping sense, psychoanalytic theory is built around the core concepts of jealousy and envy. We become who we are by jealously fearing the loss of our parents' love to siblings and other rivals, not to mention the threat of one parent stealing the other parent from us. The various machinations of the Oedipus complex offer us a matrix of jealousies and envies that ultimately form our characters. The more or less successful taming of these infantile emotional states is what socialises us. (And, as we have already suggested, different societies demand different forms of socialisation.)

Freud begins his 1922 paper, 'Certain Neurotic Mechanisms in Jealousy, Paranoia and Homosexuality', with the assertion that, 'Jealousy is one of those affective states, like grief, that may be described as normal'. Indeed, he goes further, saying that people who *don't* experience jealousy consciously will be all the more tormented by it unconsciously. Still, he tempers this by saying that conscious jealousy is far from completely rational and is liable to involve a misperception or distortion of reality thanks to its deep, infantile roots. So, for Freud, both jealousy and the lack of it are somewhat mad.

However, not all jealousies are equal. At the lowest level we find '*competitive* or normal jealousy' – the kind we seem more or less unable to live without. Next up is 'projected' jealousy, which involves accusing the other of that which one knows one is guilty. Freud matter-of-factly describes one of the great difficulties of married life: both sides know that temptation is everywhere. Still, because everybody understands how nice it can be to seduce and be seduced, there are plenty of places in normal social life that grant 'a certain amount of latitude'. The mixing up of couples at dinners, for instance. Nonetheless, there are some who refuse to see that this sort of low-level rule-bending is there to make life easier, and they insist on kicking up a fuss, projecting their 'own impulses to faithlessness onto the partner'. (Perhaps it's interesting to note here that Freud posits a kindly, tolerant social gaze as opposed to Engels's controlling, coercive one.)

At the top of Freud's pyramid of possessiveness is 'delusional' jealousy, whereby a person becomes passionately focused on tiny manifestations of their partner's unconscious to the total erasure of their own. While their interpretations may not be entirely off the mark, they are hyper-investing the unconscious of other minds in order to shield themselves from their own unwanted thoughts, in particular from disavowed homosexual attractions. It hardly seems necessary to quibble with Freud in saying that the far greater social acceptance of queerness has done little or nothing to abate delusional jealousy, which continues to ruin gay and straight relationships indiscriminately.

Phyllis Greenacre, in her 1969 paper 'Treason and the Traitor', follows Freud in seeing jealousy as universal, dating it back to the emergence of the family as a social unit. Still, if that sounds like the beginnings of an argument for the socially constructed nature of jealousy, she also tells us that, 'Animals, too, seem to show jealousy and rivalry. This is seen in the pecking order among some birds, the courting activities of many creatures, and even in the behaviour of the household pet who attacks the new baby'. Still, the outside world clearly impacts human interiority, and Greenacre uses the example of war as a trigger for treacherous behaviours. If 'doubts, hostile feelings and suspicions' might be held at bay in times of peace, war gives them an opportunity to be expressed, 'Whether it's a war between nations, or within a single nation – or, at a much simpler level, a feud between families'.

From here, Greenacre goes on to scour fragments of the childhood histories of famous traitors in order to 'discern the outlines of certain developmental character disturbances leading to deformation of the maturing ego'. She continues:

> Especially important is the invasion of emotional relationships by the excessive need for possession and power, growing out of unusually strong and unresolved infantile jealousy; distortion of the sense of identity sometimes with secondary disturbance in reality testing, and a fissure-like defect in the superego (including the conscience and formation of ideals).
>
> (p. 202)

All of which is to say that unchecked infantile jealousy can have terrible effects. Her chosen subjects provide Greenacre with a litany of absent, alcoholic, odious, and weak fathers, lonely childhoods, and one maternal suicide. In other words, these kids were not 'well socialised' according to the textbook. Therefore, their natural but objectionable infantile impulses went on to find unfortunate expression in their adult lives, not only in their relationships but also in society at large. It seems that for Greenacre, jealousy is an expression of the primal wish to control and to avoid losses. Untamed, it will potentially express itself through destructive, omnipotent acts, leading to anything from unhappy love lives to high treason.

In a footnote early in her essay, Greenacre comments on the double-edged nature of jealousy. She explains, 'In the 16th Century the word has two meanings – one of eager devotion, the other of angry indignation'. Indeed, the roots of the word in the Greek 'zelos' link it to 'zeal'. Diana Fuss brings out a similar split in *Identification*

Papers, using Lacan's opposition between the specular image and the *corps morcelé* and the fact that an identification is just as likely to make us envy or hate someone as to like or love them. She is also careful to untangle the differences between envy and jealousy, which seem surprisingly (and interestingly) difficult for many people to grasp. Envy entails wanting what someone else has, while jealousy is the fear that the one you love will be taken from you. In this sense, envy is more twisted, or sophisticated, involving a greater elaboration of self, other, and society. Jealousy invokes the risk of a direct loss, while envy involves the wish that someone else should be the loser. Whom you love or hate in this mess is a matter for your psyche to juggle. In the case of jealousy, you might hate the person who appears to be trying to dislodge you with regard to the one you love. Or you might hate your lover for their apparent disloyalty. With envy, you may seek to destroy the person who appears to have what you lack, or you may decide to align yourself with them, making of them an ego ideal.

In any case, perhaps, we might say that both jealousy and envy are feelings that erupt with regard to *having* or *not having*, which perhaps brings us back to where we began. In cultures that promote and idealise certain forms of 'having', from plentiful grain stores to SUVs – not to mention economically stable, 'happy' love lives – it's perhaps not such a leap to see how jealousy and envy might be normalised or even encouraged.

Toxic monogamy

The term 'toxic monogamy' was introduced in a Tumblr post by nankingdecade in 2016. It's been reposted over 100,000 times, and the expression itself has become a meme. Apparently, there are people who object to the concept, in the way that there are people who don't like the phrase 'toxic masculinity'; they mistakenly imagine it means that all masculinity and all monogamy are toxic, rather than designating toxic subcategories of each. Anyhow, the post has this to say:

What I mean when I say 'Toxic Monogamy Culture'

the normalization of jealousy as an indicator of love
the idea that a sufficiently intense love is enough to overcome any practical incompatibilities
the idea that you should meet your partner's every need, and if you don't, you're either inadequate or they're too needy
the idea that a sufficiently intense love should cause you to cease to be attracted to anyone else
the idea that commitment is synonymous with exclusivity
the idea that marriage and children are the only valid teleological justifications for being committed to a relationship
the idea that your insecurities are always your partner's responsibility to tip-toe around and never your responsibility to work on

the idea that your value to a partner is directly proportional to the amount of time
and energy they spend on you, and it is in zero-sum competition with everything
else they value in life

the idea that being of value to a partner should always make up a large chunk of
how you value yourself

From traditional fairy tales to Hollywood, it's not hard to see how people are
encouraged to believe in ideas like 'true love conquers all' or that straying from
one's relationship is a catastrophe for all concerned. Every day spent working as a
psychoanalyst is likely to be a day when one of the 'issues' raised in this list is also
raised in your practice. Partners of all genders will tell you how hard it is to sustain
desire in a long-term relationship, and new parents (mothers, in particular) will
fantasise about bringing their child up in a community rather than being isolated at
home (before acknowledging that the contemporary urban housing market makes
this next to impossible). The monogamous family as the economic unit of society
is indeed very often a recipe for domestic strife, precisely as Engels described.
But what is one supposed to do about it? Looking at the psychoanalytic literature,
you might conclude that the path of least resistance would be to 'detoxify' your
monogamy. Following Freud, this might involve attempting to bring your *'projective'* or *'delusional'* jealousy back to something more *'competitive* or normal'; or,
going with Greenacre, one might want to look into the distortions around identity
and disturbances in the superego. Then you will be able to work off your excess
libido at dinner parties and get on with being a functional economic unit. However,
if this all sounds obnoxiously normative, you might want to consider more radical
alternatives.

Freeing love

In southern Germany in 1978, a psychoanalyst, a physicist, and a theologian joined
forces to create a new community based on principles of truth and mutual trust.
They were disappointed in their parents' and grandparents' generations, whom they
believed had lied (perhaps even to themselves) about their activities during World
War II. They also felt let down by the revolutionary student movements of the
1960s, which had imploded due to internal conflicts. Undeterred, they set out to
build what they saw as more solid, trustworthy foundations for co-existence. They
imagined a research centre that drew in experts from the fields of architecture, food
security and new technologies, including bionics.

In 1983, having gathered 50 members, the group committed to spending
three years in isolation in the Black Forest. They went to work on social subjects
such as sex, love, and money under the motto, 'Nothing that is human is alien to
me'. In order to access the more difficult recesses of their own and each other's
inner lives, they used art and theatre, developing a practice they christened SD
Forum, 'SD' being an abbreviation of the German word 'Selbstdarstellung', meaning 'self-expression'.

Like many others of their generation, they rejected what they saw as Freud's bourgeois normativity, instead reviving the theories of the Freudo-Marxist Wilhelm Reich, who not only fully supported the sexual revolution but saw the traditional family, with its authoritarian patriarch, as the birthplace of the fascist mentality. This experimental community set out to see what it would be like to be relentlessly honest with themselves and each other about their drives, desires, fantasies, and fears, with the overarching, psychoanalytically inspired idea that truthfulness would provide some kind of salve. Of course, this quest for 'truth' was coupled with a very strong wish to create a different kind of society; hence, perhaps, a greatly increased tolerance for uncomfortable and difficult ideas. Under these very particular conditions, if your friend wanted to have sex with your lover, or your lover wanted to have sex with all of your friends, you might feel it was worth the pain if it meant a future free from fascism. Plus, if you could make a really great piece of theatre out of it, then even more people would love you and/or want to sleep with you.

What's perhaps surprising about this experiment is that it was so successful, at least on its own terms. The community still exists, having expanded to 150 people now living together in southern Portugal in a self-built village they have christened Tamera. They continue to practise both 'free love' and SD Forum. Many of the first babies born into the community still live there and are bringing up their own children, most having done time in the outside world and found it wanting. There are numerous relationship and family configurations, including a mother and a child with two fathers who are treated equally, and who refuse biological testing on the grounds that they are both the 'real' dads. Each adult has their own home (which is very often a simple caravan), although couples may choose to sleep together in each other's spaces over many years. Monogamy and asexuality are also considered perfectly acceptable options but, like all other romantic/erotic permutations, are of great research interest to the group. There are still major leftovers of heteronormativity, but the younger members of the community are working hard to correct the blind spots of the elders, including their un-self-critical Whiteness.

As part of their ongoing research, they are part of a large network of international intentional and indigenous communities who share resources and information on everything from permaculture to water retention landscapes to dealing with the emotional volatility of groups. They also host visitors whose research interests intersect with theirs, many of whom are psychotherapists and psychoanalysts – including this one. One of their many cautions to guests, who may have noted how fun and pleasant their lives appear, is not to imagine that one can go home and simply put their ideas into action. Although they take it as axiomatic that 'jealousy isn't part of love', it doesn't therefore follow that we should all go back to our towns and cities, stop being jealous, get on with practising free love, and wait for the miraculous political benefits. As they see it, the unravelling of internalised patriarchy and capitalism, along with their 'toxic' accompanying behaviours and attitudes, is a complex, agonising process that needs to be done in dialogue with others over time, and in deeply immersive situations. Without this density of opportunities for self- and other examination, you are liable to end up with the emotional hellscape known as urban polyamory, with its rules, rotas and sickening cocktail of fomo, competition, and acquisitiveness, not to mention the likely involvement of an app.

Far from implying a carelessness with the bodies and feelings of others, Tamerians see erotic freedom and true partnership as inherently compatible. Rather like Freud's dinner guests, they view multiple attractions as inevitable. However, unlike their bourgeois counterparts, they consider it perfectly acceptable to act on them. Still, in both cases an existing relationship is understood to be potentially enriched by a 'certain amount of latitude'. (Of course, one might argue that this is simply a comic case of straight people working out what queer people, thanks to their historic exclusion from traditional family and domestic structures, have known for quite some time.)

Conclusion

As a testing ground for the detoxification of human relationships, Tamera has developed quite particular methods, and these might not appeal to everyone, but it's interesting to see how a community formed almost four decades earlier has come up with elegant ways of confronting the exact problems identified by nankingdecade. While it may be true that even the family pet experiences jealousy, it's also quite clear that the containment, or not, of certain emotional states is knitted in with the ideologies in which one is immersed. At its most extreme, we might see this in social and legal systems, where it's acceptable to physically punish or even kill a woman on the grounds of infidelity; if there's no strong external incentive to contain one's jealousy, you're left with internal ones which, alone and unsupported – or even criticised and questioned – are more likely to fail. Conversely, if the rules around exclusivity in love are completely relaxed, it appears possible for people to co-exist harmoniously enough over long periods, although they may need an overarching belief system – like the idea that they are working against fascism – in order to keep their more difficult feelings in check. Still, balanced against the idea that Tamerians are merely one tiny cluster of utopian thinkers, there is their engagement in a far wider community of communities, many of whom have been honing their philosophies and modes of existence for hundreds if not thousands of years. Of course, few would want to claim that any society is perfect, but given the broadly noted discontents of this one – not to mention its devastating impact on both the earth's natural systems and on other human cultures – it's compelling to look at other psychosocial possibilities.

Reference list

Engels, F. (1884). *The origins of the family, private property and the state* (A. West, Trans.).
Freud, S. (1923). *Certain neurotic mechanisms in jealousy, paranoia and homosexuality* (J. Strachey, Trans.).
Fuss, D. (1995). *Identification papers*.
Greenacre, P. (1969). *Treason and the traitor*.
Nuñez, G. (2024). *Felizes por enquanto: Escritos sobre outros mundos possíveis*.

Chapter 3

Jealousy

Darian Leader

Although there is by now a substantial psychoanalytic literature on jealousy, it is curious how it has not attracted wider study given the fact that ownership disputes remain the main global cause of homicide. Whether violence is directed at the partner or at the rival is a clinical question that requires unpacking, just as the complex relations between envy and jealousy may be helpful in understanding both the direction of violence and the motif of possession itself.

Possession and ownership are of course at the heart of psychoanalytic theories of development. Most accounts of the Oedipus complex situate the issue of possession of the mother as a decisive factor: is she felt to belong to the child or, at a certain time, to a third party, and to whom does the child, in turn, feel they themselves belong? How do they disengage from this, and whatever the responses may be, how are these registered and inscribed?

The same goes for the supposedly pre-oedipal relations to the mother's body: to whom does the breast really belong, and how are such questions treated and transformed over the course of the first few years of life? Whether our references are to Freud, Klein, Winnicott, or Lacan, the problem of possession is ubiquitous, and it occupies a central place in all their theories, from Freud's notion of the 'injured third party' in love life, to Klein's dialectic of envy and gratitude, to Winnicott's transitional space and Lacan's scopic notion of envy and the shifts between being and having in the castration complex.[1]

*

Classical psychoanalytic accounts of morbid jealousy tended to occlude the question of possession with their focus on latent homosexuality, a problem that was compounded by the failure to distinguish between love and desire. On this model of mostly male jealousy, the jealous husband is in fact really interested in his rival, an interest that under repression gives the Freudian formula: 'It's not me that loves him, it's her'. Clinical cases show a bifurcation here, with the jealous party overtly concerned either with the rival or with the partner, to suggest that the Freudian formula may be applied, with caveats, only to the first rather than the second clinical

DOI: 10.4324/9781032637549-3

picture. This is complicated further by the narcissistic dimension that is often present in such cases, where the obsession with the rival is predicated on apparent similarities and mirroring. Freud even referred here to a "grief" about the rival in male jealousy (Freud, 1922, p. 223).

In contrast, an almost exclusive concern with the partner rather than the rival may show, as I've argued elsewhere, the effort to turn female sexuality into a sign, to make it speak or confess, a result that is at odds with how Lacanian psychoanalysis characterises women (Leader, 1996, pp. 59–62). The husband who examines his wife's underwear microscopically, counting the number of pubic hairs to try to establish correlations between these deposits and her trips outside the home, presumably aims to create an equation between her sexuality and a number. Jealous violence towards the woman to follow might then claim to be strictly based on evidence.

Such cases can easily be subsumed in the Lacanian model of phallic versus non-phallic sexuality, so that jealousy appears as the consequence of the dissonance between these two dimensions. Female sexuality never belongs entirely to a flesh-and-blood partner – whatever their gender – and the effort to appropriate it into the phallic domain of possession is constitutive of jealous thought and action (Morel, 2000). One might query here why it is jealousy rather than envy, and perhaps the reason this step has been avoided by most Lacanian commentators is the risk of association it carries with the old ideas of womb envy, mother envy, etc., that are ridiculed in our milieu. Better just to say the phallic function needs to appropriate the not-all.

Shifts in popular culture have tended to privilege either the one or the other of these approaches. The buddy radio shows of the 1940s like *Captain Flagg and Sergeant Quirt*, and then the movie comedies of the 1950s often pitched two male chums in rivalry over a woman. At the end, they'd choose each other, with the woman either abandoned or somehow shared: 'We want to marry you' as the pals propose in *Two Guys from Milwaukee*. The buddy dimension becomes eclipsed by the violence of possession in *Laura* or *The Invisible Man*, where a man's overriding need to possess a woman reaches a murderous pitch. The aim here is to negate desire entirely.

Note how, if the buddy movie triangles are less prevalent today, crime dramas have in a way taken over their function: an ex-con or crime veteran is persuaded by his old buddy to do one last, dangerous job, abandoning his partner or wife to do so. Effectively, this means choosing the male over the female party, and it is no accident that the old buddy is almost always somehow the object of an affective ambivalence: they are never the recipient of unalloyed love but of mixed feelings, a sense of debt together with resentment (Wolfenstein & Leites, 1950). Often, things end badly.

Before exploring further the theme of ownership, it is worth considering the place of the woman in these triangles. What we so often find in cases where jealousy starts to trump affection is that the male party has situated a rejected part of themselves in their partner – call it a feminine part if necessary – which basically means a part of themselves which is felt to be in the place either of a sexual object or of a sexual agent. Being a sexual object here may resonate with the primal scene, or, more generally, with how a child might imagine the mother's place in sex; and being a sexual agent tends to involve the broadcasting of appetite, a motif frequent in fairy tales where the bad queen, witch, etc., really *wants* something. Being an object and being an agent are both highly dangerous and must be negated, sometimes with tragic consequences.

This brings out a less obvious aspect of the classic Freudian emphasis on the 'homosexual' link: it may not be a love for the male rival, but a way of treating the threat of that part of one's own sexuality that is most powerfully resisted, repressed, or foreclosed, and which is housed in the image of the woman's sexuality. This is not exactly the same as an ascription of one's own unfaithful tendencies to the partner, and the inferred sexuality may remain absolutely opaque. As an analysand who was desperately jealous of his girlfriend put it, she had become 'an emblem of the life I hadn't lived'.

*

One of the most important features of Lacan's reformulation of the Freudian Oedipus is the focus on naming: there is not just separation from the mother but also an inscription of this process, a psychical designation. This implies – with a crucial modal question mark – not just the presence but the registration of a third party. In its initial formulation, it is the Name of the Father that allows a negativisation of the desire of the mother, an operation that presupposes the earlier one of a symbolisation of her absences. The tempering effects of this process revolve around the inscription of a signification of loss.

It is never suggested that the paternal metaphor here causes an exacerbation of jealous rage, presumably because this would be seen as located in the imaginary, and the metaphor treats, precisely, the polarised field of imaginary aggressiveness. It is worth remembering, however, that the paternal metaphor is not just about phallic signification but also about ownership and possession, which is one of the reasons why the signification is of loss. But if meanings like 'Her desire is directed somewhere else' or 'She's with someone else' are not crystalised into a signification of loss, they may remain an open and torturous question or accusation. Meaning is pinned down, but this has an aggravating rather than a tempering effect, with the presence of a third party either not occurring or occurring but not registered. It is a clinical question why such torsions of the paternal metaphor can stay latent for so long and then emerge in old age, with jealous accusations and reproaches so common in care and retirement homes.

One of the problems with our Lacanian approach here is the way that it tends to shoehorn together early triangulations and the later donor functions of the Oedipus complex. A year-old baby may well have managed to symbolise the 'operation of the mother's absences', but it won't be for quite a while that the question of having or not having the phallus is treated. Confusing these two processes is ill-advised, and results in obscuring exactly what we need to distinguish in the clinic of jealousy. The third party linked to maternal absence may be registered or not, but if it is, this does not guarantee that the symbolic function of the gift will be accepted or that later exchange circuits will be inscribed. It is unlikely that a one-year-old expects a baby from the father, just as it is unlikely that trust is not established way before the paternal metaphor.

The consequence here is a differentiation of third-party positioning. If this has not been registered in relation to maternal absences, there are at least two options: the partner's absence is felt as a dreadful and tormenting open question with a rival at the horizon, and the subject searches desperately for proof, for meaning – we would say meaning in the place of the missing phallic meaning – or, on the contrary, the third party is appealed to in a resolutive way: absence is treated by imagining a third party, and hence those cases in which jealousy is tolerated and even encouraged.

This is different from the neurotic triangulation which allows a question to be posed. A woman may be jealous of another woman in her partner's orbit as a way of articulating the question: 'What does she have?', 'What makes her the object of love/desire?'. Similarly, a man may require another man's interest in a woman in order to make his own feelings seem definite, just as the image of a woman can moderate the intensity of men's feelings for each other. In Jules Dassin's *Brute Force*, the male prison inmates tolerate their own homoerotic proximity thanks to the poster of a female pin-up on the cell wall.

The next differentiation presupposes kinship registration, and anthropological studies show how kinship structures have effects on the distribution of jealousy. This may be more likely, for example, from uncle to father in matrilineal societies than in patrilineal ones, where jealousy of a son's respect for his father is perhaps unusual. It is often pointed out that familial functions traditionally separated between at least two figures – such as affection and interdiction – are combined in the modern nuclear family, so that one single person must act as the agent of two arguably separate schemas.

Myth and folklore show this separation, with the donor figure almost always distinct from the father, who may be kind, harsh, or indifferent but, crucially, does not give his son the instruments necessary to complete his tasks or mission. More often than not, he in fact sends his son away to find his own path with nothing. The instruments are then bestowed by another figure, a donor, visible today in the Q figure in the James Bond films, the giver of magical objects that have the power to kill one's enemy. Note how the donor operates in both male and female oedipal trajectories here, with the gift of a child still quite firmly inscribed in the unconscious within those societies in which patriarchy is challenged.

It is also quite striking how myths and folklore seem to divide a legitimate and an illegitimate appropriation of the gift. If Q gives his gadgets willingly, other mythological characters use guile or threat to obtain them, a differentiation that echoes the clinical picture in neurosis, where the subject may complain of a sense of not owning what they have, and this perhaps has effects in the field of jealousy. In his classic 1936 study 'Jealousy and Sexual Property', Kingsley Davis pointed out not only that it is a mistake to see jealousy as a triangle, but that the legitimacy or illegitimacy of the rival will play a significant part in the affects felt. One may legitimately compete with a rival to gain possession of a partner, but if one achieves a socially sanctioned ownership position – such as marriage – the rival now becomes a trespasser, and violence against them is deemed acceptable and encouraged in many cultures.

*

Davis's reading of jealousy in terms of property conflict may seem both callous and exclusively patriarchal, but it brings out exactly the terrible claims at the heart of love and affective relationships. The four variables in the jealous 'quadrangle' for Davis are the owner, the object, the rival/trespasser, and the public. This last element must be included in order to grasp the social character of jealousy and how it can be shaped differently in different cultures. Rivalry, for example, may be absent if the competing party belongs to a certain social class and exacerbated if they belong to a different one, since each society distributes its sexual property in different ways.

A sexual act between one man's wife and another man may be socially sanctioned in some circumstances in one social group yet prohibited in another. What appears to be the same act may be felt as ownership in one social context and as robbery in another, as the 'giving' of a wife to another man may assert the owner's status as owner in some cultures at some moments, and at other times constitute theft. The same sexual act may generate quite different emotions accordingly (Clanton & Smith, 1977, pp. 114–158).

The relations between the four variables for Davis will differ depending on whether the conflict situation is one of regulated competition (for example, suitors) or illegitimate trespass (for example, adultery). Crucially, he distinguishes between ownership and possession, since property is not always in the hands of the owner even if it is so legally, and possession may occur despite – or even because of – an owner. The danger regarding one's elected object is that someone else will win out in legitimate competition or that someone will take what they feel belongs to them, so trespass. Society tends to encourage fear and hatred of trespassers but to suppress that of rivals, and if a rival persists after the victor has fortified their claim, they become a trespasser.

Ownership without custody is common in sexual life, as is possession without rights, and affection itself can be owned but not possessed. Many people, as Davis observes, remain faithful to their partner despite having little affection for them, just as they may choose fidelity while never having sex. So far, so good, but the property model is complicated by the fact that the attitude of the object will play a dynamic part in the equilibrium: if the partner obstructs or actively seeks another person, this will no doubt have effects. Davis notes here what Ernest Jones and other analysts at that time had missed in their focus on the blow to self-esteem in jealousy (Jones, 1929): that in these situations, the owner is identified with the object, so that '"Mine" becomes "I"'.

The implicit reference here is probably William James's famous observation that the 'Me' is predicated on what is considered 'Mine', creating an identification that is inherently fragile given the fact that one's possessions can be appropriated by others, damaged, or destroyed (James, 1890; McDougall, 1926; Belk, 1988). This in turn can be used to generate schematic distinctions between envy and jealousy: any figuration that presents an image of total possession of an object can inspire envy, whereas jealousy involves the attitude of the object towards a third party – in other words, desire and agency.

This is a neat distinction, but it is hardly comprehensive clinically, as jealousy may contain an envy, just as envy can fracture into jealousy. For Klein, the motif of possession here actually dispenses with a possessor, as it is less a question of a mother possessing a breast than a breast possessing and gratifying itself, to generate an envy that the addition of operators like a possessor or a depriver in fact mitigate and treat (Klein, 1957, pp. 183, 198). Klein's careful work on the relations between envy and jealousy – and on how jealousy may involve a working through of envy – is well worth revisiting today and remains more subtle than the broad brush-stroke distinctions we tend to make as Lacanians, where the split is often just another way of allowing us to retain the false dichotomy of the relation of the subject to the object (a) or to the Other. This has the unfortunate effect of obscuring how relations to the object may contain links to the Other, and vice versa.

Another way to approach the problem here would be to link jealousy to ownership issues and envy to possession: that is, how someone else is imagined to possess something. The complexities of the links between envy and jealousy could then be explored through the question of the relations between ownership and possession, from the nursery right through to the priority disputes of academics and inventors.

*

What can a psychoanalytic approach add to Davis's model here? Perhaps the most obvious point is that the clinic of jealousy shows a breakdown or an exacerbation of this social theory of jealousy. Tensions with a rival and obsession with a trespasser can go beyond socially accepted limits, just as a rival may be experienced as a trespasser without any socially reinforced justification. There is an excess here that torments and may even destroy the jealous party, and that may lead to violence towards one's rival or one's object. Rather than seeing this in simplistic quantitative terms – 'an excess of jouissance' – we can understand it in terms of the consequence of the non-inscription of a third-party function, which then makes other problems – such as dealing with another human being's sexuality – much more difficult.

A further issue with the property model is its apparent restriction to male jealousy, yet this is not entirely the case. Many of Davis's points are applicable also to female jealousy, and in a sense would be all the more so given that this is a social theory, and that sex roles are largely social constructions. Yet this would also invite us to rethink some of the well-known binaries distinguishing between male and female jealousy (Baumgart, 1990). For example, to say that a jealous man will not ask for details about what his rival looks like but is much more likely to ask what he does, whereas a jealous woman will want to know what their rival looks like could be seen as precipitates of socialisation processes which put a premium on female appearance and male achievement, etc. As socialisation processes change in some parts of the world, one might wonder what effects there might be on the formal properties of jealousy.

And also, on what might prove less susceptible to change. Take for example the dynamics of female friendship groups in adolescence. Much of the agony of these years is a result of sudden and unexpected reconfigurations of the principal ties within the group, and the loss of best-friend status. What the reconfigurations so often have in common is the effort to remove one party from another party, to seize possession of someone who was possessed by another member of the group. A hasty reading of such dynamics would posit an oedipal template: the girl tries to win one parent away from the other, and she enjoys her victory if she succeeds.

Although this may have a purchase in some cases, the key is surely the prising away, the breaking up of one intimacy to create another, so that to some extent the value of the object lies in its previous tie to the other party. But what kind of victory is this? Is it just an affirmation that one's own value exceeds that of the 'injured third party', to use Freud's expression? Someone has been taken away from someone else, and is now part – or all – of what one has. This in itself is a definition of what an object is in psychoanalytic theory, but the question is whether this is an oedipal process or a more archaic one linked to earlier object relations, or – why not? – a combination of the two (Klein, 1957, pp. 197–198).

For Joan Riviere, the substructure of jealousy here is envy, based on the effort to rob the mother of her possessions and rendering her destitute (Riviere, 1932). Enjoyment is linked to despoiling and depriving others, to maintain the image of the robbed and injured mother, a consequence of oral envy, whether this takes as its object penis or breast. The term 'jealousy' is preferred to 'envy', she argues, as this appears more ego-syntonic, and it is the oral basis of envy that explains the greater incidence of jealousy in women, as their libidinal development is more closely linked to oral libido.

To take a recent example, we might ask what the goal was of the Emma Stone character in *The Favourite* in replacing Rachel Weisz in the affections of the Queen. Was her aim to become the favourite of the Queen, or, on the contrary, was it rather to prise the other favourite away from her, to remove the latter's power and appropriate it herself? The Queen herself doesn't seem so important in all of this except as the receptacle of what it is that needs to be prised away. Is the aim to replace or to remove, or perhaps simply to destroy the favoured object? These are hardly one and the same psychical operation, and it would seem equally implausible to imagine that the goal was, to follow Riviere's model, the creation of a lack in the Queen.

The immense, immeasurable popularity of the *Daily Mail* celebrity feed shows this process in action. Readers from all social strata enjoy the tarnishing and fall of those whom society had previously favoured, to create a sense of relief: not a lack in the Other, but a spoiling and removal of the Other's object. As Susan Isaacs observed, 'it matters more to deprive the other person of what he has than to have it oneself' (Isaacs, 1946, p. 224). The process here seems more important than the particularity of the object itself. But what exactly is the process?

*

The separation here is less between the Other and the object than between the subject (the Favourite) and the object: spoiling means that they are deprived of their possession of the object, a desecration that may well have an oral rather than a scopic substructure, as Klein and her students believed (Klein, 1957, p. 183). So effectively ownership and possession are split apart, a dynamic that is sometimes seen as a characteristic of female sexuality and, as we've noted, is ubiquitous in the reconfigurations of adolescent groups. This is presumably the real stake of the proposition in *The Story of O* to break the subject from their sexual jealousy towards their lover, to allow a new kind of eroticism from which the quest for possession barred them.

Yet this is also a motif in male sexuality, with an inverted focus: less to split ownership and possession than to try to solder them together. At one level, this permits a simple oedipal reading. Possessing requires a registration to transform it into ownership, yet the oedipal story involves the failure of both of these projects (in relation to the mother) in return for the promise of future possibilities (with others). What is registered is not ownership but the failure of possession, accepted with greater or lesser difficulty by different subjects, and generating a variety of sexual permutations in later life: for example, to offer inadvertently or deliberately one's partner to others, to exert excessive control over them, to engineer losing them, etc. In this context, note how the plea for sexuality beyond jealousy in *The Story of O* might just constitute a consolidation of male phantasy: the woman can be used like a chess piece without too much protest.

But the basic oedipal trade-off complicates matters. In the Lacanian schema, the phallus is available for future use, but note how the phallic model of having contains implicitly a non-phallic dimension. The boy must renounce being the phallus in order to have it, yet since the phallus is a signifier – or, as Jung put it, the symbol of abstraction – it can never be entirely owned: it will always be a having which includes a not-having, which is one of the reasons why the spectre of bodily damage and loss is always so pervasive (Lacan, 1958). Although the phallus can never be fully owned, it may be available on loan or leased out, and it is perhaps not an accident that both Freud and Lacan use this vocabulary of property arrangements to describe the psychical situation here.

The implication is that however normative the passage through the Oedipus and castration complexes might be, jealousy remains as a residue and a potential due precisely to this non-ownership at the heart of ownership. The space created by this dissonance can easily be occupied by images of another man – or woman – as the phallic image is refracted. But the dimension of the object – and hence perhaps of envy – is situated in the relation between the other two parties, crystalising the subject's exclusion.

So to conclude, we can distinguish a variety of forms of jealousy: those issuing from a problem in the registration of a third party in the efforts to 'make an operation of the mother's absences', and those linked to later oedipal dynamics which involve the more overt motifs of possession and ownership. Within both of these spaces, we can find a mobilisation of what is most probably the experience of an archaic oral exclusion, where the subject feels that someone else possesses and enjoys an object – which must hence be torn away from them and destroyed. Happy times!

Note

1 Note that Lacan's first publication in a psychoanalytic journal was a translation of Loewenstein's study of jealousy, 'Un cas de jalousie pathologique', in the *Revue Francaise de psychanalyse*, 1932.

Reference list

Baumgart, H. (1990). *Jealousy*. University of Chicago Press.
Belk, R. (1988). Possessions and the extended self. *Journal of Consumer Research, 15,* 139–168.
Clanton, G., & Smith, L. (Eds.). (1977). *Jealousy*. Prentice Hall.
Davis, K. (1936). Jealousy and sexual property. *Social Forces, 14,* 395–405.
Freud, S. (1922). Some neurotic mechanisms in jealousy, paranoia and homosexuality. In *The standard edition* (Vol. 18, pp. 223–232). Hogarth.
Isaacs, S. (1935). Property and possessiveness. *British Journal of Medical Psychology, 15,* 69–78.
Isaacs, S. (1946). *Social development in young children*. Routledge.
James, W. (1890). *The principles of psychology* (Vol. 1). Holt.
Jones, E. (1948). Jealousy. In *Papers on psychoanalysis* (5th ed., pp. 325–340). Balliere. (Original work published 1929).
Klein, M. (1975). Envy and gratitude. In *Envy and gratitude and other works* (pp. 176–235). Hogarth. (Original work published 1957).
Lacan, J. (2006). The signification of the phallus. In B. Fink (Trans.), *Ecrits* (pp. 575–584). Norton. (Original work published 1958).
Leader, D. (1996). *Why do women write more letters than they post?* Faber and Faber.
McDougall, W. (1926). *An introduction to social psychology*. Methuen.
Morel, G. (2000). Feminine jealousies. In R. Salecl (Ed.), *Sexuation* (pp. 157–169). Duke University Press.
Riviere, J. (1932). Jealousy as a mechanism of mechanism. *International Journal of Psychoanalysis, 13,* 414–424.
Wolfenstein, M., & Leites, N. (1950). *Movies, a psychological study*. Free Press.

Chapter 4

Sisterly jealousies

Geneviève Morel

Translated by Kristina Valendinova

Robert Siodmak's thriller *The Dark Mirror* (US, 1946) tells the true story of twin sisters who do everything together; they live together and even share the same job without anyone realising. They seem to love each other deeply, but everything goes wrong when one of them receives a marriage proposal. The man is murdered. We know that one of the sisters is guilty while the other has a perfect alibi, but which one is which, given that they refuse to tell? New York state law stipulates that two people cannot be convicted of the same crime if one of them might be innocent. To tell the suspects apart, one of them would have to let herself be trapped, caught red-handed, or made to confess. The police are helped by a twin specialist, who believes that not everyone can commit a crime and that he can discover the culprit using psychological tests. The tests suggest that one of the sisters is mad and dangerous and the other isn't, but again, which one is which, given that when interviewed by the psychiatrist, the jealous killer passes for her sister? She convinces her innocent twin that it is in fact *her* who is mad and guilty, and has forgotten all about her crime. Not even love can help the doctor make the call, when he identifies the sister in question through a kiss yet doesn't know whether she is innocent or guilty. However, this puts him in mortal danger, which finally helps the police crack the case.

Jealousy between sisters has been the topic of a number of other films, some of which border on the horror genre; for example, Robert Aldrich's *What Ever Happened to Baby Jane?* (US, 1962). Baby Jane is a gifted child actress who sings and dances, managed by her father, a failed actor. Her entire family lives off her brilliant success, especially a sentimental song in which a girl professes her love for her dead father, as well as a line of porcelain dolls made in her likeness. Her stern older sister Blanche has no such charisma, but she too is talented and works hard to become an actress. Gritting her teeth, she tolerates the whims of the spoiled and obnoxious Jane, whom their father grants her every wish, while bullying Blanche and always siding with her younger sister, who in turn publicly humiliates her. A scene at the beginning of the film shows young Blanche's deep-seated hatred when she sarcastically replies to her mother's request to remember, once she grows up, to be kinder to her sister than the latter is to her now: 'You bet I won't forget!'.

DOI: 10.4324/9781032637549-4

As an adult Jane becomes an alcoholic, forever fixated on her childhood doll-like image and her love song for her father, who has since passed away. Blanche, who in the meantime has become a star, keeps her promise and takes care of Jane despite the latter's antics. But her career ends abruptly when she's injured in a strange car accident, which she blames on Jane. Suddenly Jane has to take care of Blanche in her beautiful house and uses the opportunity to treat her with great ambivalence for many years. The true horror begins when Jane, now an ageing alcoholic terrified that Blanche would institutionalise her, kills the housekeeper and tortures her sister. She mimics her sister's voice on the phone to prevent a doctor from visiting, forges her signature to access her bank account and shuts herself away in a delirious world of Baby Jane, with her doll and her dead father. The end of the film is terrifying. Before she dies, Blanche confesses to Jane that it was she who had caused the car crash: she had wanted to kill Jane who had mocked her at a party, but the plan backfired and she herself ended up paralysed. She had been lying all this time to take revenge on Jane and make her feel guilty. But for Jane, it is too late; she has sunk into complete madness.

The childhood rivalry between the two sisters, fuelled by their father, therefore ruins the future of the younger sister and triggers the hateful jealousy and stubborn resentment of the older one. Bound together by a hatred that is not without its emotional ambiguity, they end up destroying each other.

In these films, the jealousy between the sisters is inseparable from an omnipresent play of mirrors, as the original title of the first film, *The Dark Mirror,* suggests. *The Dark Mirror* also reminds us of the argument developed by Lacan in his 1938 paper on *Family Complexes*, which concerns both brothers and sisters. An 'intrusion complex' develops for young children who have a sibling close enough in age which can be very powerful, especially for the older sibling, who loses their 'privilege' when another child is born.

Lacan comments on the scene described by Saint Augustine in *Confessions*: 'I have myself seen jealousy in a baby', Augustine writes, 'and know what it means. He was not old enough to talk, but, whenever he saw his foster-brother at the breast, he would go pail with envy'.[1] The scene involves three characters: the mother, the child we suppose is being breastfed, and the one observing, who experiences a feeling of extreme and unique bitterness – jealousy or envy, depending on the translation – that I will call *invidia,* even though Lacan doesn't yet use the term in this text.[2]

A few initial comments. First, the intrusion complex is not a vital competition, a struggle for survival, because the child observing has already been weaned and no longer needs to be fed in this way. Instead, it is an identification contemporary to the formation of the ego during the mirror stage. It is based on the observing child's identification with another child, which comes after the lived experience, because this child too had previously experienced the jouissance of his rival at the breast. Second, this identification is facilitated by the similarities in terms of age, stature, and body image. Lastly, what is characteristic of *invidia* is precisely this commingling of love and identification, which engenders aggressivity as a consequence: 'The sight of the unweaned sibling evokes aggression only because it recalls the imago of the maternal situation and its concomitant death wish' (Lacan, 2001, p. 37).[3] The death wish has already entered the subject as a consequence of weaning and the child's longing to find again the lost imago of the primordial mother.[4]

While Lacan strips *invidia* of all moral naturalistic judgement à la *homo homini lupus* and instead describes it as an imaginary and sociocultural mechanism, its complexity and lethal substrate nevertheless raises the question of crime: 'In this way, the non-violence of the primordial suicide engenders the violence of the imaginary murder of the sibling' (Lacan, 2001, p. 40).

In Aldrich's film, the hatred between Jane and Blanche as adults does not efface their infantile ambivalence of love and identification. Jane in particular continues to love her sister and to imitate her even as she is killing her. And the structure of the scene in which Blanche is looking at her little sister dancing with their father while everyone applauds recalls Augustine's scenario. Her gaze and gestures already betray the *invidia* that later provoke her murderous attack on Jane.

Lacan's identificatory sketch complicates the narratives of evil twins that populate fantasy literature and emerge unexpectedly only to kill. Later in the text, the intrusion complex, which should be – but isn't always – resolved through the Oedipus complex, becomes associated with behaviours such as showing off, seduction, domination, subjugation, and sadomasochism.

Lacan was interested in how the elder child, traumatised by the arrival of the younger 'intruder', could overcome the fraternal complex. The 'vicissitudes of the ego' of the older sibling depend on the developmental moment in which the complex emerges. Early on, the spectacle of the younger child's enjoyment which reactivates the 'disruption caused by weaning' can lead to schizophrenia, hypochondriacal neurosis, or 'the imaginary destruction of the "monster"', which results in perverse drives or obsessional guilt. But when the younger child arrives after the older sibling has entered the Oedipus complex, he is accepted following the patterns of parental identification and 'aggressive drives are sublimated into tenderness or sternness' (Lacan, 2001, p. 44).

This optimistic picture of Oedipus as a cure must nevertheless be somewhat qualified. Especially in the 'passion of romantic jealousy', where the 'original ambiguity' (Lacan, 2001, p. 39) – of love and identification – in *invidia* is reactivated in the fascination with the rival, often concealed by obsessional hate. Lacan mentions the psychotic forms of this passion, where 'maximum aggressiveness' 'stems much more from the denial of this unique interest than from the rivalry that supposedly justifies it'. While he seems to return to Freud's theory of projection in paranoia (Freud, 1911, p. 63) (*It is not I, but her or him who loves*), he draws different conclusions from it, making a direct link between the violence of aggressiveness and psychotic negation: the foreclosed refusal to recognise one's own fascination with the rival is what drives the jealous person to the very extremes.

The intruder

I seem to have found this characteristic negation at the origin of the crimes committed by Lucie D, whom I met after her latest offence: she had stabbed to death Adel, a mentally ill man 20 years her junior, who lived under her guardianship.[5]

Lucie had met Adel, her young neighbour living with his mother, during a period of unemployment. They began an ambiguous relationship as both lovers and friends, although Adel 'didn't care about sex' and Lucie couldn't get him to move in with her. Adel was on disability allowance and worked at a vocational rehabilitation centre. It was on his suggestion that Lucie agreed to become his guardian, to help him save on fees. The guardianship judge gave his consent, and Lucie was meant to meet with him shortly to present her financial report after the first year of guardianship.

Adel's betrayal

Lucie was therefore in charge of the young man's budget, which was a source of conflict. Adel would constantly lie to her to obtain more money (the sums were strictly limited by the supervising judge). Yet he still managed to save up and buy himself a nice car (which Lucie had to drive since he didn't have a permit) and was planning to buy a little fishing shed. But the judge refused. Moreover, there were some rather opaque issues with Adel's bank accounts. Lucie's role was not that clearly defined and this alone made her uncomfortable.

But beyond these financial problems, Lucie seems to have been deeply affected by a 'betrayal'. While she was still hoping they were going to live together, she found out about Adel's affair with 'a lady' whom he supposedly asked to move in with him. Lucie had seen this on Facebook, and apparently it 'had been' confirmed to her. 'I'd done so much for him and I just couldn't understand'. 'Someone' had also told her that the other woman was married.

The day of the murder – which she insists had not been premeditated – Lucie was cleaning her son Colin's house while he was at work. She then had a 'flash, an impulse', a sense of 'overwhelm'. She took a kitchen knife and put it in her bag: 'It wasn't to hurt him but to scare him. I knew *I'd been betrayed by him*, because of that woman and other things, but I didn't know by what'. She asked Adel to meet her nearby, at her daughter Ida's place. They met on a bench and again started to argue about money: Adel reproached her for giving him only 20 euro per week. She replied that, contrary to her advice, he had been stupid enough to rent an expensive flat. He wouldn't hear anything and continued asking for money. She suddenly felt 'strange', 'saw red': although she can remember only the first stab, she in fact ended up stabbing him 50 times. She then rang her ex, Mr K, with whom she was still living, for help. When Mr K arrived, they threw Adel's phone away (were there any compromising recordings?). She went home to shower and carefully washed her clothes. She cried all through the night. It was only the next day that she told her daughter Ida, in whose garden the police later found Adel's body. The knife disappeared but was later found, but not the mobile phone. The murder could have been reclassified as premeditated – carrying a heavier sentence – because Lucie had arrived at the scene with the knife she had previously taken from her son's home.

A father betrayed

Adel's murder is curiously entangled with the presence of Lucie's children and her family history. Her narration highlights the ubiquity of betrayal in her life.

Her father and mother were factory workers, and Lucie was their oldest child. Her mother had an affair with a neighbour and became pregnant with Lucie's youngest sister Jeanne, whom Lucie calls her 'half-sister', even though her father recognised Jeanne as his own. Curiously, Lucie presents this fact as a secret and, when asked about it, says that only her mother had told her about it, which seems contradictory given other details related by her. Officially, the neighbour became Jeanne's 'godfather', and her mother asked Lucie, who was 12 at the time, to be the godmother, in order to, Lucie assumes, buy her silence.

Jeanne was her parents' favourite and thus the object of intense jealousy for the rest of her siblings. Yet in the different interviews, Lucie systematically denies this. For example: 'My mother always treated us differently. She used to say I was jealous. That's not true'. Or, 'My sister would say I was jealous. Also, she was my goddaughter'. Sometimes this is a more precise denial, when in the same sequence she confirms what she has just refuted: 'My half-sister got a house and a car. My mother used to say I was jealous of her. I wasn't jealous of her. That's why I left at seventeen and a half'.

The little sister was doubly spoiled, by her biological father and her parents. She quickly inherited her biological 'grandmother's' house. The godfather then 'got together' with another woman, and they built a house opposite the parents' house. It seems as if they all lived together contentedly.

Except that Lucie describes a childhood haunted by arguments. Her father, who had been betrayed and was jealous, would drink and 'overturn tables'. He did so out of anger, and Lucie took 'all of it on herself', she says, without any metaphoric intention. Moreover, she had been 'touched' by the 'godfather', her mother's lover, and told her mother only much later (after 30 years). There was no reaction. As a teenager, Lucie took care of her brothers and sisters and later got a factory job, handing her pay over to her parents. She was in permanent conflict with her mother, the 'traitor', and maintained a degree of complicity with her father, though they didn't see each other a great deal: 'We used to go to the garden to take care of the chickens and in the evening we used to drink mint tea. That was our thing. I never got any affection'.

Early on, Lucie thus took on her father's cause and, like him, felt betrayed by her mother, who 'did not treat her children equally', and by her 'half sister', who benefited from this preferential treatment. The latter's parents gave their daughter everything, while depriving themselves on her behalf, at the cost of their other children and Lucie in particular. On top of that, when the betrayed and unhappy father drank, she would be on the receiving end of his rage.

Acts of violence

As a result, betrayal remained the leitmotif of Lucie's life. At age 17, she had had enough; in order to leave home, she got married. She had two children: Ida and Arthur. Seventeen years later, her husband became severely depressed and had to be hospitalised. But he didn't want to return home. One day, she came to visit him at the clinic with their children, where she found him at the cafe with another woman: "I didn't accept it. I had been faithful to him for 17 years." After this second betrayal, she asked for a divorce.

She then met the father of her third child, who was well established and already had a child; they stayed together for five years. They loved each other, but their happiness was eventually destroyed by the rivalries of their older children. One day, Lucie threatened him with violence (she only wanted to scare him); he was terrified, and they split up. She was given custody of little Colin.

Now aged 39 and already the mother of three children – Ida, Arthur, and Colin – she began a new, ill-fated relationship. Her new partner had a nephew the same age as Colin, and she babysat both children in order to 'help out'. One day, when her oldest son Arthur was at the house, things 'kicked off' and the nephew got smacked. It must have been a severe punishment, because he had bruises all over his body and his father pressed charges. Lucie was sentenced to nine months of prison for harming a child and Arthur, who was still a minor, received a suspended sentence.

On leaving prison, Lucie picked up Colin from her mother's. It's interesting to note the sophisticated terms in which she describes the episode: it was an 'error of justice', because though she had not harmed *her* children (but *only* her partner's nephew), she wasn't allowed a visit from them in prison. In this way, Lucie maintains a certain level of ambiguity about her criminal offence and ultimately believes that she was not really guilty. After Lucie returned home, she had a row with her mother, who had been looking after her children while she was doing time, apparently because her mother had 'played favourites' with her granddaughters and been unfair towards Colin. Of course, this preferential treatment was to benefit Lucie's half-sister and *her* children. But with each complaint, Lucie explains that she was cross with her mother and *not* her half-sister – a new instance of denial?

Her envy towards her half-sister nevertheless remains acute, as well as her sense of betrayal by her mother. Lucie also threatened to take her mother to court if she refused to help her. Their separation was definitive.

A helpful beautiful soul (belle-âme)[6]

Lucie found a job (first as a nursing assistant, then a kitchen help and an elderly care assistant), then married again. Mr K was a divorcee and an alcoholic, plus he turned out to be pathologically jealous. She broke up with him and divorced him, but they remained close. At the time of Abel's murder, she was still living with her ex-husband and having meals with him. He felt controlled by her and, when questioned by the investigating judge, Mr K apparently also accused Lucie of hitting him – this puts her in a blind rage.

Lucie had a notebook where she wrote down her interpretations and thoughts for the judge. She actively prepared for hearings and the court case; she suffered from constant nightmares about the murder, as well as regrets of her action: 'I wanted us to live together, I wanted love. It was him who loved me'. However, given the coldly detached and factual way in which she speaks about Adel's death, this remorse makes little sense.

What strikes the most about Lucie's life is the number of repetitions. First and foremost, the repetitions of violent actions: she committed two violent crimes, first against a child and then against a young disabled man. In both cases they were persons in her care. Lucie presents herself as someone who since childhood had been taking care of her siblings, helping her parents, working on everyone's behalf. When she speaks about herself, the word 'help' [aid] constantly repeats: maternal assistant, nursing assistant, household help, elderly care assistant. Helping is her vocation. She wanted to 'help out' the parents of the little boy whom she physically disciplined alongside her son; she became Adel's guardian to sort him out; she stayed living with her second husband Mr K to support him. So, Lucie presents herself as a beautiful soul, but in fact she is violent, to the point of having killed a vulnerable person who had fallen into her hands. Her only association with this is her father's fury, who would 'flip tables' during his drunken fits of jealous rage, when her mother rejected him and preferred to see her lover.

There is also the repetition of the alleged cause of Adel's murder: betrayal – an endless betrayal, one that started long ago when the mother cheated on Lucie's father with her neighbour, and then continued when her father preferred the daughter that wasn't his own, thus destroying the little bit of intimate space that Lucie had found with him as a child. The unfair treatment from her parents never stopped, whether it concerned money (she considers herself de facto disinherited) or care for the grandchildren (where her sister Jeanne would always receive more). Lucie had gone as far as taking her parents to court.

By the way, she also recently wanted to press charges against her own daughter – who had not invited her for Christmas, while she did extend the invitation to her parents-in-law – to demand the right to visit her grandchildren. She had also fallen out with Colin, despite him being her closest child, when he had threatened to stop seeing her if she started drinking again. Lucie was thus betrayed by her mother, her father, her first husband, and finally by Adel.

The maternal thing

Adel's murder was in fact motivated by a double betrayal. He made her fail as a guardian. But perhaps Lucie's reasons to take on the guardianships had other motives as well: she obtained access to a new car and might have hoped to live with him in the little house, the purchase of which had been refused by the judge. Most importantly, however, he betrayed her with another woman.

Her feelings of betrayal are very old and, as we have seen, go as far back as the birth of her youngest sister Jeanne, of whom she had been especially jealous (being the oldest child, she had nevertheless already had other siblings who had not provoked this sense of intrusion). Could we thus reconstitute the chain of events? It seems that she had been jealous of this sister, who had enjoyed too many privileges, and consequently felt a great deal of anger against her mother and identified with her betrayed father. But the situation is even more complex.

On the one hand, Lucie cannot recognise her *invidia*. Nevertheless, her *hat-eloving* (*hainamoration*) (Lacan, 1999) of her little sister, who was also her god-daughter (whom she both admired and hated), was unanimously emphasised by those around her. The hate that is denied returns as a boomerang from the outside, marking the foreclosure of her interest in her rival, the severity of which Lacan emphasises. This initial foreclosure is expressed in Lucie's speech: her negations ('people said I was jealous but it wasn't true, I have no complaints') and her denials ('I wasn't jealous, but that's why I left home'). This foreclosed fixation on her rival is the seed of the uncontrollable violence that would be triggered later, in any situation of rivalry or betrayal – just think of the rage it takes to stab someone 50 times. We should also note that Lucie says she felt betrayed by Adel, but without knowing exactly what the object of this betrayal was, despite giving us two separate reasons. This is because the ineffable sense of betrayal harks back to past dramas.

On the other hand, Lucie could not endorse the paternal cause and form a block with her father against her mother and her mother's lover, as we have seen in other family psychodramas, because her father recognised Jeanne and kept his wife. He would also spoil Jeanne and, worse still, the father's rage against his wife, fostered by alcohol, was in the end directed at Lucie.

The foreclosed fixation on her sister made it impossible to create an oedipal identification with a moderate father who would have loved all of his daughters equally; it prevented Lucie from sublimating her hateful fixation on her sister. To the contrary: it reinforced it by incorporating the father's lawless violence (the overturned tables directed at her), while Lucie also inherited his love of alcohol.

Lastly – as she explicitly says – the first traitor was her mother, having betrayed both Lucie's father and Lucie herself. Here there is no foreclosure. Mother, whom Lucie was trying to help, must have been her first object of love – a disappointing one – and the following traitors, too, were her love-objects. Throughout her life, Lucie took her revenge, but it went much further than just overturning tables. In her murderous attacks against her love-objects, wasn't she ultimately trying to kill this original mother, one who had been loved but was a bad mother?

For Lacan, the mother can be the Freudian thing, *das Ding*, the embodiment of both the ultimate enjoyment and ultimate evil in each one of us (Lacan, 2015, p. 43). Sometimes we find it on the outside: intimacy turns into extimacy, provoking horror, like the mother in Hitchcock's *Psycho,* both internal to the son and exteriorised as a killer. Norman Bates becomes his dead mother and kills young women as if he was his mother, out of jealousy and in order to prove her passionate love for her son, wishing to remain the only woman in his life.

In a manner that is of course quite different, Lucie too becomes her betrayed father, who takes revenge, striking the bad mother, the thing embodied by Adel, the most recent traitor. But Lucie also carries this treacherous mother, whom she hates with constancy within herself and therefore can't quite get rid of her. This is evidenced by one striking detail, namely that she managed to unconsciously implicate her three children in her crimes – by accident, she says. Her oldest son Arthur committed violence against a young child alongside his mother; then she got Colin and Ida mixed up in Adel's murder by borrowing Colin's knife as a weapon and leaving the body in Ida's garden. As if in committing these crimes, she did so also as a mother; and her children have not forgiven her.

Conclusion

In my 1986 essay (Morel, 2000), where I was interested in female jealousy as depicted in literature and case studies of neurosis, my key reference was the concept of the phallic not-all of jouissance. I came to the following conclusion:

> [M]asculine jealousy is an expression of a man's impossibility to *have* a woman, who is not-all. Female jealousy derives from the fact of *being*, as a woman, not-all when it comes to jouissance. 'Jalouissance' or *invidia* is imprinted on it on an imaginary level.

It is now clear that, rather than the pas-tout described by Lacan or Freud's favourite *Penisneid* (Freud, 1925), it is *invidia*, the commixture of love and identification fraught with future aggression, that appears to be the early and solid foundation of the sisterly jealousies we examined in this chapter, where at least one of the sisters is psychotic. The phallic dimension either does not exist or cannot overcome the violence of *invidia*, which is no longer just imaginary but made real by the foreclosure.

The case of Lucie D also shows us a trait we frequently find amongst female killers: their inability to separate themselves from their mother, from the 'maternal thing' devouring them from the inside, which eventually pushes them to the worst extremes, in an effort to rid themselves of it.[7]

Notes

1 Saint Augustine, *Confessions*, I, 7, quoted by Lacan (2001, p. 37).
2 Augustine doesn't use the term *invidia* but *zelans*, which means jealous or envious. Lacan later uses the term *invidia* when commenting on this passage, which emphasises the function of the gaze and which he differentiates from jealousy. Envy/*invidia* comes from observing the other's completeness which the subject has already lost, and therefore it is desperate and hateful. Jealousy aims at possessing a good we wish to have or we fear losing (Lacan, 2018, p. 115).

3 Transl. note: the English translation of *désir de la mort* by 'a death wish' is ambiguous, because it connotes something that the subject conjures or experiences at a particular moment in time, addressed to someone else; for Lacan, the desire for/of death is something that exists in the subject herself, a deathly or suicidal tendency that results from the weaning – see the following note of the author – and becomes an aggressive impulse towards the rival only when this rival presents herself at a later stage.

4 In his 1938 article (pp. 34–35 of the French edition), Lacan in fact distances himself from a biologising understanding of the drive and specifically Freud's death drive, by using the cultural notion of a 'complex' that 'compensates for a vital insufficiency by regulating a social function'. The social function of the weaning complex is thus to separate the child from the mother, which cannot be reduced, despite its name, to the contingencies of the end of breastfeeding. This complex tries to make up for the 'premature separation that is the origin of a discontent that no maternal care can compensate for', via an unconscious representation, the imago of the mother, which will be 'sublimated', so that the child can evolve in a family larger than the mother-child dyad. However, this image becomes linked to an archaic condensation of pains experienced during childbirth and later the suffering of early infancy, which comes to dominate the entire human life. The desire for death is the result of the subject's resistance to extricate herself from this overly absorbing image, and it is reactivated with every developmental crisis, as a tendency to return to it as a kind of refuge. Lacan sees the symptomatic expression of this desire that originates in the weaning complex in the various non-violent oral forms of suicide (anorexia, addictions), while motherhood is on the contrary a satisfying possibility to 'saturate' the maternal imago by its reversal into embracing and feeding the infant.

5 In France, a guardianship is a legal measure intended to protect a vulnerable adult and his or her assets. It allows them to be advised and/or supported in taking important actions (such as taking on a loan or selling a property). At the same time, the person remains autonomous in carrying out simple daily actions (everyday shopping, choosing to get married, etc.). For more info, see https://www.servicepublic.fr/particuliers/vosdroits/ F2094.

6 The Beautiful Soul is an expression borrowed from Hegel, which denotes the position of the one who bemoans the world's disorder, in which they are nevertheless doing well, unable to see precisely how their own actions contribute to its sorry state.

7 Cf. Morel, G. (2024). *Tueuses. Cinéma et Clinique*. ERES.

Reference list

Freud, S. (1911). Psycho-analytic notes on an autobiographical account of a case of paranoia (Dementia Paranoides). In *Standard edition* (Vol. 12). White Press.

Freud, S. (1925). Some psychical consequences of the anatomical distinction between the sexes. In *Standard edition* (Vol. 19, pp. 248–260). The Hogarth Press.

Lacan, J. (1999). *On feminine sexuality the limits of love and knowledge: The seminar of Jacques Lacan, book XX: Encore*. W.W. Norton.

Lacan, J. (2001). Les complexes familiaux dans la formation de l'individu. In *Autres écrits* (pp. 23–84). Éditions du Seuil.

Lacan, J. (2015). *The ethics of psychoanalysis: The seminar of Jacques Lacan, book VIIb*. Taylor & Francis.

Lacan, J. (2018). *The four fundamental concepts of psycho-analysis*. Taylor & Francis.

Morel, G. (2000). 7: Feminine jealousies. In R. Salecl & S. Zizek (Eds.), *Sexuation: SIC 3* (pp. 157–169). Duke University Press.

Chapter 5

Jealousy as a social bond

Renata Salecl

Jealousy is often taken as an individual's feeling; however, it has an essential social dimension frequently overlooked in psychoanalytic studies. On the one hand, jealousy is a necessary mark of socialisation, which is why the way we deal with jealousy, how we express it or suppress it, is very much marked by culture. On the other hand, jealousy is also exploited by ideology. Consumerism, for example, effectively plays on jealousy by enticing people to shop. And racist, sexist, and nationalist ideologies profit both from jealousy and envy related to the perception that others enjoy at our expense. Envy and jealousy towards others are, however, often perceived in a somewhat paradoxical way. We like to label migrants as lazy and, at the same time, claim that they are stealing our jobs.

While jealousy and envy are often used interchangeably, jealousy is frequently linked to intersubjective relationships which involve a possibility of loss (i.e. we might be jealous of someone who is our potential rival). Some thus define envy as a dyadic relationship (a person and something the person would like to have), and jealousy as a triadic relationship (a person and a rival who might take something from the person).

The Israeli philosopher Aaron Ben-Ze'ev sees jealousy as something very personal, something that makes us more vulnerable than envy.[1] The French psychoanalyst Claude Rabant,[2] on the other hand, describes jealousy as a murderous emotion – after all, in law we talk about murders motivated by jealousy. Some take jealousy as the more primary emotion, from which envy branches out,[3] while many psychoanalysts view envy as a more aggressive emotion than jealousy. When we are jealous, we may wish to have something that others have, or not to lose what we have, but when we are envious, we might not wish to have what others have, but rather hope to destroy the pleasure that we think the others are getting from something. Suppose we feel envious when we see that our neighbour has bought a sports car. We may not be interested in such a car, but we find it hard to see the pleasure our neighbour gets from driving it, and so we may fantasise about the possibility that the car gets wrecked.

This chapter will look at the social dimensions of jealousy and envy, and their relationship to the desire of the Other. It will question how both jealousy

DOI: 10.4324/9781032637549-5

and envy have been incorporated into authoritarian political systems and how they have been exploited at moments of social crisis, like the COVID-19 pandemic.

Jealousy and the question of who I am for the other

Jealousy does not necessarily emerge only when people have direct contact with each other. We might be jealous of people we have never met, and even dead people might incite this strong emotion. For several years, a woman I will call Maria dated a man I will call Joe. Maria spent the weekends with Joe, taking care of his apartment, buying provisions for him, and enjoying their journeys by car to neighbouring villages. Joe engaged in many creative pursuits but rarely made any money. Maria worked hard and lived frugally while being generous towards Joe and paying many expenses. When Joe's old car broke down, Maria immediately came to help and bought a new one. Having a car was essential for the weekend trips the couple liked to make; however, it was Maria who covered most of the costs related to these outings. While Joe appreciated Maria's generosity, he was often moody in her company, critical of her dress style and lack of education. Joe's bad temper and depression became more pronounced when his creative pursuits brought no social recognition or financial success. Maria ended the relationship after eight years of enduring this somewhat turbulent partnership.

Joe and Maria continued to be friends; they saw each other once or twice a year, and occasionally, Maria still helped Joe cover his expenses. The friendly relationship, however, ended when one day Joe asked Maria for money for a new computer. Maria was eager to help and offered Joe an old computer she had at home. Joe, however, insisted that he wanted a new one. In anger, Maria left Joe's apartment and stopped communicating with him.

A few years later, when Maria learned that Joe was dying, she went to visit him in the hospital. They had a few lovely hours together until a woman (I will call her Linda) appeared in the room and presented herself as Joe's wife. Linda explained that she knew Joe as a student and that in the last year, they reconnected as friends and became especially close when Joe fell gravely ill. Linda and Joe married in hospice, and in the previous weeks of Joe's life, Linda spent most of the days near his bed, taking notes about what he wanted to do with his estate. When Joe died, Linda took over Joe's state-owned apartment, organised his affairs, and connected with Joe's friends from many avenues of his life.

After Joe's death, Maria fell into a deep depression. She could not stop crying, could not eat, and felt terrible guilt for not being more attentive to Joe when he fell ill. But most of all, Maria started experiencing extreme jealousy towards Linda. The fact that Joe and Linda got married just before Joe's death was, for Maria, a betrayal. She started remembering how Joe never wanted to move in with her, how he always exploited her financially, and how critical he often was towards her. Maria began to be haunted by the question of who she was in Joe's life when they were a couple.

Money started playing an essential role in this question. The jealousy towards Linda increasingly circulated around the idea of profit. Maria regarded Linda as someone who primarily wanted to profit from Joe's death; however, simultaneously, she started calculating how much Joe profited from her in the past. Maria was jealous that Linda would now possess some objects that she bought for Joe; however, when Linda offered Maria the car and anything else she wished from Joe's meagre possessions, Maria refused. Her jealousy was not related to what little Linda might profit from her late husband, but to the symbolic recognition that Linda received by marrying Joe.

When Joe was alive, Maria never regretted splitting up with him. It was only after Joe's death that old wounds opened up. Although Maria had a reasonably comfortable life in the house she owned, she detested the idea that Linda moved in with Joe in the last weeks of his life and took over the lease of his apartment. Maria refused to come to the memorial Linda organised for Joe and hated hearing the news of how Linda started promoting Joe's work with the help of social media. The fact that Linda was keeping Joe somehow symbolically alive after he was physically gone was for Maria hard to observe. The rival took over Joe's afterlife. And, suddenly, Maria had to deal anew with the question of what role she had played in this dead man's life.

Jealousy and ideology

People can experience a particular kind of jealousy regarding the question of what role they play in society. In societies where success relies on finding a way to cheat the system, jealousy is often a way people express their anger not at the system but primarily at their lack of success in circumventing the rules. In this situation, the rivals have found a way around the regulations more successfully and have thus received a better social status.

Such jealousy has been observed in several countries that underwent social transition after the collapse of socialism and have ended up in authoritarianism, such as Russia. At the start of the new millennium, Russian journalist Masha Lipman[4] questioned why most people in Russia were so apathetic and did not resist the autocratic regime that had formed under Putin's tutelage. Lipman's thesis was that many people in Russia took for granted that they live in a hostile world where the authorities are corrupt and care only about themselves and little about the people. Because you have no hope that the system will change, as an individual, you have to constantly look for holes in the system, try to trick the system, pretend, cheat, steal, and lie. Lipman points out that the post-socialism system in Russia quickly began to function similarly to socialism. Leaders always lie and do not expect people to believe them. In response, people lie to both the authorities and each other. Stalinist terror has taught them not to trust anyone and to pretend to be loyal to anyone. However, behind this pretence is a desire to circumvent the rules, find the holes in the system, and profit when finding a way around the social prohibitions.

For the late Russian sociologist Yuri Levada, the founder of public opinion research in Russia, who had problems in both Soviet and post-Soviet times for his analysis of people's attitudes towards power, the main feature of the mentality that developed in their country was cunning. The Soviet man seemed passive and submissive, but there was something defiant about that attitude. The apathetic people were anarchic; even though they seemed to act as if they were blind to how the regime was working, they were wise and resourceful regarding cheating the system.

When the Soviet regime collapsed, and there were no more old bans and walls around which an individual would look for detours, the previous curtains behind which people hid their little cheating also fell. Levada, therefore, says that in post-socialism, cunning has become overt. After the end of the Yeltsin regime, the dream that the country would turn in the direction of democracy was quickly shattered. At that time, people became even more cynical; distrust of each other increased, and at the same time, there was a rise in jealousy of those who had succeeded economically. The latter were perceived as people who were more cunning than others.

In a country where it is no longer a secret that lies and cheating lead to success, apathy on the outside looks like a lack of interest in the political struggle, like accepting that authoritarians will be in power forever. In private, however, the individual is even more active in seeking ways to outwit the system and his compatriots. When people deal with how to be as cunning as possible every day, they have no respect for the successes of others – the latter are perceived as better fraudsters, more immoral, and crueller. One might be jealous and envious of such people, but one would not respect them.

When people expect nothing more than fraud, they are not ashamed when they are cunning. However, they become angry with themselves when they are too cynical or when they become too idealistic. Jealousy in this case paradoxically functions as something that pacifies people, helps them to conform to the way the system functions, and prevents them from seeing the broader picture of the system in which they live.

Jealousy and the pandemic

At the time of the COVID-19 pandemic, one could also observe jealousy that was linked to whether others were finding ways to ignore the rules and were having an easier time with the lockdowns. When the COVID crisis started in 2020, people were hearing that we were all in the same boat because the virus can kill indiscriminately. Since access to health services and testing, and the possibility of isolating oneself, had an impact on morbidity and survival, it soon became clear that the boats people found themselves in were very different. One might find oneself in a perforated dinghy while others enjoyed lockdowns in their yachts.

In France, the writers Leïla Slimani and Marie Darrieussecq aroused public outrage when they described in newspapers their daily lives in their lavish weekend houses in a rural part of France. Slimani[5] wrote in *Le Monde* how she had enjoyed beautiful nature with her children, how she woke up every day with a view of the hills, and how she told her children that it was like the story of *Sleeping Beauty*. Darrieussecq confessed in *Le Point* how on arrival at her holiday home, she hid her car with its Paris registration plates in the garage and started using a rickety old vehicle with a local registration plate so as not to anger the villagers.[6] Both writers spiced up their writing with photographs of views of unspoiled nature from their quarantine residences. When many other wealthy people started posting photos from their weekend homes on Instagram, a whole barrage of criticism began on French social networks: poor people started posting pictures of views of walls and dilapidated houses from their small-town apartments and blogging about what family life was like in a couple of square feet of living space. Jealousy and anger towards the rich led some villagers in France to write public posters saying, 'Don't bring us your viruses', and 'Go back to your cities and take the virus with you'.

American writer Leslie Jamison describes her feelings of jealousy and envy, which emerged when she found herself infected with coronavirus while taking care of her young daughter as a single mother. She struggled with the disease and, at the same time, did her best to deal with her little girl, who was unstoppable in her desire to get to know the world. Exhausted from the virus, Jamison read her daughter stories about rabbits, bears, snakes, and sheep for the hundredth time, while the child enjoyed spreading cream on the floor and watching her exhausted mother clean it up. 'The virus is my new partner', Jamison wrote, 'our third companion in the apartment, wetly wrapped around my body at night'.[7] After waking up soaked with sweat, she could barely stand on her feet during the day. One day, she became jealous and angry when, looking through the window, she saw four high school students walking hand in hand. Jamieson read the scene as if the students were signalling to the world: We don't care about the rules. While Jamison was tempted to yell out of the window at the reckless youngsters, she realised that moralising about people's disregard for social distancing instructions was actually a way for her to deal with her own fears.

In Slovenia, just before the government restricted people's movement to their home municipalities, the media competed to catch people walking on the beach or the shore of the Alpine lakes. On television reports, viewers watched people sitting on benches and even a group supposedly having a river picnic. However, the same footage kept popping up, and it became clear that the camera operators were deliberately filming people to look as if they were walking in a group, not individually or as part of a family. The discourse that accompanied the tightening of quarantine rules strongly emphasised the problem of enjoyment. The idea was that some enjoy at the expense of others. Some were diligent and locked in apartments, while others walked on the beach. It was as if the media deliberately encouraged jealousy and envy so that angry viewers would not object to rather random and often contradictory rules that the government imposed at the time of the lockdown.

Sigmund Freud, in his work 'Group Psychology and the Analysis of Ego',[8] connects social justice with forming a group spirit, when people perceive themselves as equal and when no one stands out because of who they are or what they have. For Freud, this demand for equality is the foundation of social consciousness and a sense of duty. Social justice means that we deny ourselves many things so that others may be without them or so that they will not be able to demand them. As Freud points out, this idea of social justice stems from envy. He takes the example of people infected with syphilis who are afraid of infecting other people. Their fear, according to Freud, is associated with an unconscious desire to spread infection to others. These patients are wondering why only they should have been infected and cut off from the world, and why this horror is not happening to others as well. Freud's thesis is that forming a group spirit reverses these hostile feelings towards positive social ties that lead the individual to try not to infect others.

This reversal often occurs in a group under the influence of emotional ties with the leader, who is perceived as both part of the group and somehow outside of it. In his study of groups, Freud highlights the example of the military and the church. Identification among group members is tied to the feeling that the leader treats everyone equally. When the leader privileges one over the other, the identification between the group members collapses. In the case of a group of soldiers, such a collapse of the structure can also increase feelings of anxiety.

Suppose we implement the Freudian theory of the groups in societies facing the coronavirus. In that case, we can observe that when the leaders in many countries started privileging themselves at the expense of others or helping their friends profit from the pandemic, this affected the group spirit in these societies. If, at the beginning of the crisis, there was a strong call for solidarity and the proclamation that we were all in the same boat, it quickly became apparent that many of those who were supposed to be captaining the ship were primarily taking care of their own interests. And it is not surprising that with the end of the belief in a common goal came new forms of aggression, as well as an increase in anxiety.

Conclusion

In the Russian language, envy is often explained in two different ways: white envy and black envy. The interpretation is that white envy entails the pain of a felt lack (for example, of wealth, youth, or strength), and a wish and yearning to have or regain what the other enjoys without wanting to destroy it or him or her. Russian-American journalist Masha Gessen perceives white envy as an inspiration for 'I want to be you'. In contrast, black envy hints, 'It should be me, not you'.[9] Black envy is mean and resentful. It affirms a despondent worldview, while white envy offers a hopeful one.

White and black envy exist also at the level of society. Gessen takes the example of the 2014 Ukrainian Maidan revolution, which forced authoritarian pro-Russian leader Viktor Yanukovych out of power. Observing the success of the Ukrainian protests provoked white envy among many Russians who wished that such uprisings would also take place in Russia, where Vladimir Putin was increasingly cracking down on the opposition and taking all power into his own hands. Gessen wrote at the time that, unlike black envy, which in Russia usually confirms a despairing view of the world that does not expect anything good in the future, white envy, in the face of the uprisings in Ukraine, gave Russians hope for the possibility of change in their country. This hope was lost in the next years, however, and the country increasingly embraced black envy. The attack on Ukraine in 2022 was its explicit expression. The fact that Ukraine was turning away from Russia, trying to build a democracy, independent culture, and identity, provoked anger in the Kremlin as well as fear that something like that could happen in Russia.

While envy can sometimes lead to actual violence and destruction, jealousy might also have positive effects. Birmingham ethics professor Kristjan Kristjansson[10] argues against viewing jealousy as a negative emotion. He says that in some places in the past, jealousy has been seen as a sign of an irredeemably corrupt mind, or at least of an overly possessive and insecure character. Some psychologists have written of jealousy as a pathological condition that needs to be treated. Jealousy was also perceived as something that did not promote compassion for one's fellow man. However, there is also a perception that envy is worse than jealousy, since it is associated with a more negative view of others than jealousy. In his defence of jealousy, Kristjansson stresses that jealousy is not necessarily a virtue but should be seen as one. Jealousy is linked to the desire for recognition and respect, which is why it is fundamentally a social emotion.

Throughout history, many psychoanalysts have addressed when jealousy and envy arise in a child. These emotions have often been linked to when a child acquires a sibling. Jacques Lacan[11] put forward the thesis that jealousy is a critical moment in the child's socialisation because, on the one hand, it helps the child to identify strongly with someone, while on the other hand, it allows the child to cope with someone else's desire. With jealousy, we realise that it is not only us who have desires, but also others.

While envy and jealousy are often looked upon negatively, they are essential to socialisation. It is through jealousy that we recognise that we question desires of other people and also the Lacanian Big Other. Jealousy confronts us with the question of our lack and the lack in the Other. With envy, however, we can get motivation to make something out of our lives.

Envy can also be an encouragement at the level of society. When countries observe the direction of other countries, there is a difference in the type of envy they develop towards them – destructive black envy, or white envy, which motivates positive social change.

Notes

1 Ben-Ze'Ev, A. (2001). *The subtlety of emotions*. MIT Press.

2 Rabant, C. (2015). *Jalousie*. Éditions Gallimard.

3 Tor-Zilberstein, D. (2023). *Jealousy, femininity and desire: A Lacanian reading*. Palgrave Macmillan.

4 Lipman, M. (2005). Apathy into anarchy does go. *Index on Censorship, 34*(4), 52–56. https://doi.org/10.1080/03064220500429783

5 Slimani, L. (2020, March 18). Le 'Journal du confinement' de Leïla Slimani, jour: 'J'ai dit à mes enfants que c'était un peu comme dans la Belle au bois dormant,' *Le Monde*. https://www.lemonde.fr/idees/article/2020/03/18/le-journal-du-confinement-de-leil a-slimani-jour-1-j-ai-dit-a-mes-enfants-que-c-etait-un-peu-comme-dans-la-belle-au-bois-dormant_6033596_3232.html
6 Darrieussecq, M. (2020, March 20). Nous planquons au garage notre voiture immatriculée à Paris. *Le Point*. https://www.lepoint.fr/culture/marie-darrieussecq-nous-planquons-au-garage-notre-voiture-immatriculee-a-paris-19-03-2020-2367952_3.php
7 Jamison, L. (2020, March 26). Since I became symptomatic. *The New York Review of Books*. https://www.nybooks.com/daily/2020/03/26/since-i-became-symptomatic/
8 Freud, S. (1953). Group psychology and the analysis of the ego. In J. Strachey (Ed.), *The standard edition of the complete psychological works of Sigmund Freud* (Vol. 18). Hogarth Press and the Institute of Psychoanalysis.
9 Gessen, M. (2013, December 2). A whiter shade of envy. *New York Times*.
10 Kristjansson, K. (2001). *Justifying emotions: Pride and jealousy*. Routledge. https://doi.org/10.4324/9780203165881.
11 Lacan, J. (2020). *The seminar of Jacques Lacan, book IV: The object-relation (1956–1957)* (A.R. Price, Trans. & J.-A. Miller, Ed.). Polity Press.

Reference list

Ben-Ze'ev, A. (2000). *The subtlety of emotions*. MIT Press.
Darrieussecq, M. (2020). Locked down in paradise. *Le Point*.
Freud, S. (1921). *Group psychology and the analysis of the ego*. Hogarth Press.
Gessen, M. (2012). *The man without a face: The unlikely rise of Vladimir Putin*. Riverhead Books.
Jamison, L. (2014). *The empathy exams: Essays*. Graywolf Press.
Kristjánsson, K. (2018). *Virtuous emotions*. Oxford University Press.
Lacan, J. (2002). *Écrits: A selection* (B. Fink, Trans.). W.W. Norton & Company.
Levada, Y. (2004). *Soviet man and post-Soviet man*. Levada-Center.
Lipman, M. (2005). Russia's path to autocracy. *Foreign Affairs*.
Rabant, C. (2010). *L'ombre portée de l'autre*. Éditions de l'Olivier.
Salecl, R. (2011). *The tyranny of choice*. Profile Books.
Slimani, L. (2020). Diary of confinement. *Le Monde*.

Chapter 6

Jealousy of the real

Akshi Singh

There are some lines by Annie Ernaux that have become my companions. They live inside me, and I find myself reaching for them often. They are more a puzzle than a comfort, and what follows is an account of how they came to occupy such a place. But first, the lines. This is from *The Possession*: 'Now he's in the bed of another woman. Maybe she makes the same gesture, stretching out her hand and grabbing his cock. For months, I have had a vision of this hand and have felt that it was mine' (Ernaux, 2008, p. 8). And this, from *Simple Passion*: 'When I was a child, luxury was fur coats, evening dresses, and villas by the sea. Later on, I thought it meant leading the life of an intellectual. Now I feel that it is also being able to live out a passion for a man or a woman' (Ernaux, 2022, p. 48)

I was on the phone with a friend in the Biography section of a large bookstore. It was quiet, there was a good phone signal, I was unlikely to be overheard – all of which were important because I was confessing to her my ill-judged romantic desires. The conversation shifted to Annie Ernaux's *Simple Passion*. I told her about the relief I had felt on reading it, a relief that came from discovering that the consuming, maddening, irrational quality of a love affair could be brought into language, that it was possible to survive both passion and its aftermath, to lose all sense of one's own self and somehow find it again, albeit changed and reconstituted. *Simple Passion* is the distilled account of the author's love affair with a foreign diplomat – married, often unavailable. The author's desire for this man is consuming – it renders other parts of her life tiresome, all her time is oriented towards him. She lives when they meet, at other times, she waits: 'After he had put on his jacket, it would all be over. Now I was only time flowing through myself' (Ernaux, 2022, p. 16).

I would have loved *Simple Passion* for its account of the affair alone, but in the last few pages of the book, we find not just a depiction of passion, but a depiction of writing about passion. And then, as now, I was preoccupied with writing and how to sustain it, with the distinction between writing and living, not least because all too often I felt – and still feel – that I am living most when I am writing. But having agreed to write this essay on jealousy, I found myself struggling to find anything to say on the topic. I began to resign myself to the fact that perhaps

DOI: 10.4324/9781032637549-6

I would need to apologise and withdraw from the project. The problem, if it could be called that, was that of late, jealousy had been absent in my life, or so I thought. Which is not to say that I wasn't dissatisfied, frustrated, annoyed, or troubled by things. But I wasn't suffering from jealousy, and I felt this way because after years and years – what felt like an entire lifetime – of wanting to write but lacking the confidence to step fully into this desire, I was finally writing. Like most explanations that are obvious and consoling, this one too would prove to be inadequate, but I didn't know better then.

I had nearly completed a book. It had been difficult, but something about the difficulty had been absorbing and sustaining. Although there were all kinds of things I wanted, like clothes, money, holidays, something about being able to wake up and write made these things which I wanted but didn't have feel somehow less consequential. Other, deeper desires were also unfulfilled – I wasn't a mother – but that too felt bearable in a way that it may not have done otherwise. Every time I tried to think of jealousy, I felt only its absence in myself. I am ashamed to admit it now, but at times I thought, with hubris I didn't even know myself capable of, that maybe I had somehow *solved* jealousy – not for other people, but at least for myself.

At the end of our phone call about *Simple Passion* and fraught desire, my friend recommended Ernaux's book on jealousy. She said it was extraordinary; it took feelings that were too shameful to admit and put them into words. In that conversation, as at most other times in life, I have taken for granted the association between jealousy and shame, the way in which a confession of jealousy – and more often than not, an account of jealousy is framed as a confession – is accompanied by forms of disavowal and distancing. But as soon as I wrote this, I wondered if jealousy becomes particularly shameful only when self-possession is an ideal, a prized quality of behaviour and social deportment. And there was something smug about my perceived absence of jealousy, and the equilibrium and self-containment it made possible.

Annie Ernaux's slim book of memoir, *The Possession*, is set in the aftermath of a separation. It is after the author has bid goodbye to her lover – 'I was the one who had left W, several months earlier, after six years together – as much out of boredom as from an inability to give up my freedom, reclaimed after eighteen years of marriage, for the shared life he so strongly desired from the start' (Ernaux, 2008, p. 8) – that jealousy arrives. It is the knowledge that her lover is in a new relationship that marks the onset of jealousy, which takes root as a form of possession: 'the existence of this other woman took hold of me. All of my thoughts passed through her' (9). I read the book with the same absorption with which I had read *Simple Passion*, but something about the jealousy Ernaux invokes on the page remained abstract.

I tried to think back to my earlier, prolific experiences of jealousy, to try to find a way into thinking about the topic. I recalled the times when I had envied people's homes, families, lovers, jobs – the corrosive sensation of jealousy, like acid reflux, the way it took hold and somehow made the things that were missing the most important things, the determining fact in how I read my life and that of others. Or in Ernaux's words, the way in which jealousy 'transforms every difference into a lack' (Ernaux, 2008, p. 43). I thought too of the question that I would sometimes ask myself – am I jealous, or am I envious? But the distinction didn't make sense; the two inevitably folded into each other – other people, by having what I didn't have, were also dispossessing me of something that I maybe did, or could have had – happiness, peace of mind, inspiration – and then I was jealous of what may have been mine, but had been taken away by the sole fact of the good fortune of others.

I could remember these feelings, but I couldn't *feel* them in a way that would allow me to turn them into questions I needed to investigate. In learning to write, I had realised that I could only really write from a position that was mine, and by this I don't mean I could write only in the first person, just that it had dawned on me that my writing was as much connected with what was missing and messy in my life as with what was stable and consoling. I wasn't in a rush to want other people's lives, because I didn't know how I would write from the inside of these enviable lives. I still felt pangs of jealousy and envy nearly every day, but they didn't take hold in the way they had done in the past. I realised that my envy and jealousy presumed a field of equivalences between people, an endless, comparative hell, and I noted with satisfaction that I had found my freedom from such a place.

Such moments of equanimity, this freedom from troubling emotions – it does not last.

I finished my book, I went to another city to see friends. Walking down the street, I saw two people – both of whom I desired, and had reason to hope that they returned my desire – standing intimately together. I had known them, for the most part, separately. It was late, it was dark, everything around and inside me lurched. I couldn't not look, I couldn't bear to look. I turned around and walked away, unable to make sense of what I'd seen. Leaning alone against a wall (my legs no longer felt they could support me), I saw them again before me, they stepped indoors. I could still see them through a pane of frosted glass, the colours in which they were dressed blurring into each other, the pigments merging and separating. Once again, I started to walk away, once again I couldn't *not* look. I turned around. Through another window I saw the same two people standing ever so slightly apart, I saw a fist closing upon a handful of hair.

***

Where jealousy is, it seems imagination is close at hand, it may even *be* the hand, for instance in the line from *The Possession*, quoted at the start of this essay. After her lover starts a relationship with another woman, Ernaux describes becoming consumed by an urgent desire to know the details of this woman's life – her name, what she looked like, where she lived, how she dressed: 'I was no longer the subject even of my own fantasies. I was being inhabited by a woman I had never seen' (Ernaux, 2008, p. 16). Being separated from the lover she previously found tiresome is now painful. She is haunted by him, by memories of their time together: 'I wanted him *back*' (Ernaux, 2008, p. 19). She begins to understand how people go mad and commit acts of violence: 'I became accepting of behaviours that had formerly been stigmatised for me or that had provoked my ridicule' (Ernaux, 2008, p. 29).

Jealousy raises the most harrowing questions about where an object belongs, its proper place. And then, to all the anxiety accompanying that question is added another excruciating twist of the knife: can an object even belong? It introduces disarray into an order we have taken for granted, thus revealing to us the arbitrariness of our assumptions. The subject of jealousy is a displaced subject – or rather, a subject who has had revealed to her that she was always displaced, never really in charge, certainly not the mistress of her own house. Is the subject in possession of the object, or possessed by it? In alerting the subject to its inability to control, or own the object, jealousy sends her searching, landing her in places she didn't expect to be. In wanting to possess something – a lover, some information about a lover's lover, the person experiencing jealousy is herself possessed – 'in both senses of the word', as Ernaux reminds us. Jealousy strikes at the root of the subject's fantasies of her own independence and rationality; it exposes her frailty to the inconsistency of the other. Wanting something for herself, the subject of jealousy can longer even be certain if she belongs to herself.

Ernaux's style is epigrammatic, fragmentary, but its pointillist depiction of jealousy brought to mind the great and detailed study of jealousy in Proust's *In Search of Lost Time*. The narrator's pursuit of Albertine, the object of his desire, is an agonising portrait of jealousy. The narrators of both *In Search of Lost Time* and *The Possession* become consumed with the particulars of the people they desire, enacting baroque schemes to find the information they feel they must have and cannot live without. Both find themselves traversing the city: 'The strangest thing about jealousy is', Ernaux writes, 'that it can populate an entire city – the whole world – with a person you may never have met' (2008, p. 15).

But what does the person experiencing jealousy want to get hold of? Both Proust and Ernaux seem to suggest that it can't be the desired object itself. Marcel is bored when he has Albertine, he finds her dull and tiresome. As the poet Anne Carson puts it in *The Albertine Workout*, Marcel 'equates possession of another person with erasure of the otherness of her mind, while at the same time positing otherness as what makes another person desirable' (Carson, 2014, p. 9). It is a situation where the cure for jealousy means the destruction of desire. Ernaux herself is unconvinced that she wants her lover back in the quasi-conjugal arrangement that she first rejected: 'if he were suddenly to say "I'm leaving her and coming back to you," after a minute of absolute happiness – of almost unbearable elation – I would feel an exhaustion, a mental depletion comparable to that of the body after orgasm, and I would wonder why I had wanted this thing' (Ernaux, 2008, p. 54). Moreover, she continues her sexual relationship with him even after the start of his new relationship, suggesting once again that jealousy is not a response to a straightforward absence that can be remedied by renewed presence.

We could instead wonder whether jealousy is connected to the possession of knowledge – maybe knowledge that has been eroticised by its connection with the desired object. In wanting to know where Albertine goes, who her friends are, whether she really desires women more than she fancies men, Marcel is perhaps trying to solve something about the enigma of the other's desire. Jealousy introduces passion into knowledge; it gives it a magical quality, the power to end the suffering that comes from the other – 'I absolutely had to know her name, her age, her profession, her address', Ernaux writes of the woman in a relationship with her lover (Ernaux, 2008, p. 10). Or, as the psychoanalyst Anne Dufourmantelle writes, wanting to 'know everything' becomes a way of obtaining a 'sign that, finally reassured, we could rely on the other', immediately reminding us that 'it is precisely here that the illusion begins' (Dufourmantelle, 2021, p. 103).

***

Looking at the couple from which I was excluded, I felt assailed by the primal scene, plunged into an abyss of doubt, sick with feelings of abandonment. It was jealousy. *Were* they a couple? What had I seen? It was the *Urszene* of exclusion. Could I believe my eyes? What did this mean – for what I knew of them, for who I thought they were? The two, previously held separate in my mind, congealed into one. And what did this mean for me, and what I wanted? Confusion, questions, a feeling of being shut out. Now I could remember jealousy, and all its torments. I felt as though I was in possession of but a handful of pieces from a puzzle, but arrange and rearrange them as I may, I could not ascertain its shape, let alone find a solution. I was suddenly and entirely convinced that purgatory was a real place, because I was in it, I was in *limbo*, in the sense that I felt suspended in torment without reprieve.

And in that moment jealousy felt like a very old feeling, that it had always been there, in the shape of an old, old fear – of being forgotten, a confirmation that I didn't matter in the way in which I had hoped. In the days that followed, I repeatedly experienced a sensation comparable to waking up suddenly in the middle of the night from a dream – except this happened when I was awake, and I realised that these shocks were the sign that my fabric of reality was having to restitch itself around a tear, through which appeared questions I did not know how to answer. The city became a gaping wound; it was haunted by what I had seen and therefore carried the threat of exposing me to further unwelcome sights, and at the same time it held out the hope that I may find in it clues to help me understand what I had been confronted with.

Jealousy is a reminder, not just of the forms of pleasure and enjoyment that we don't have access to, but also of the more unsettling knowledge that the people we love and desire the most passionately are unknown and unreachable, they have secrets, they are unfulfilled, and sometimes they are happier when we are not around. And that these unreliable, unavailable others are all mixed up in us, so when we lose them through their absences and betrayals – both everyday and extraordinary – we also lose ourselves. In 'Mourning and Melancholia', Freud wrote about the way in which the state of melancholy involves not just the loss of the other but an '*identification* of the ego with the abandoned object'. The melancholic bemoans both what she has lost, but this lost thing is also inside her, it is part of her, the 'object-loss' is also an 'ego-loss' (Freud, 2001, p. 249). Jealousy too, is the site of such a mix up between self and other, and this lends it the recalcitrant, recursive quality so familiar to anyone who has suffered its pains.

Centuries before the publication of Freud's essay, Robert Burton made an association between jealousy and melancholy in the early seventeenth-century text *The Anatomy of Melancholy*. Bringing together classical and contemporary sources on the topic of melancholy, Burton dedicates a part of his book to a discussion of jealousy, telling his readers that jealousy has sometimes been taken as cause and sometimes as symptom of melancholy by other sources, but due to the 'latitude' and 'prerogative' of jealousy ('so furious a passion, and almost of as great an extent as love itself'), Burton himself gives it an eminent place in his book (Burton, 2001, p. 257). After considering in turn the jealousy of tyrants and elephants as presented by Burton, it was a relief in my jealous state to find him concluding that women aren't more jealous than men; it is just that the melancholic are prone to jealousy, and it is the jealous who are melancholic. As to the cures for jealousy, Burton finds the common refrain amongst his sources that the conditions for jealousy cannot be avoided, and that those who act on their jealousy or turn to violence or control are misguided, and find no relief. Jealousy can only be alleviated and tolerated; it can't be done away with.

After finding herself sympathising with the crimes of Othello, and fantasising about killing the woman she is possessed by, after imagining herself wooing her lover back, and further attempts to discover the identity of the woman, Ernaux too comes to a conclusion not too different from Burton's – there is nothing to be done with jealousy, except bearing it. Unlike Marcel in Proust's novels, Ernaux is not in a position to make a prisoner of her lover. Gender and economics play a part (nothing suggests that she has the means to hold another person captive in her apartment), but she is also able to listen to her lover when he says he doesn't like being pressured. Ernaux doesn't conflate her search for the desire of the other with control of an actual person. The jealousy, its consequences – these are hers, they are her problem, and not those for which her lover can be made to pay the price, though this feels impossible to accept, and therein lies much of the suffering of jealousy: the other can't be known, and can't be controlled.

***

The relief, when it came, was simple to the point of absurdity.

After days of suffering and anguish, of calling friends and telling them the same story they had already heard, first with interest, then with boredom and dismay, I found myself alone one evening. The prospect of being by myself was suddenly terrifying. So far, following Burton's suggestion, I had surrounded myself with friends. To find myself alone on a weekend evening was confirmation that every-one else – in the entire world, my jealousy would have me believe – was engaged in pleasure to my exclusion. I felt immune to distraction, and time was moving very slowly. Eventually, because I could not think of anything else to do, I pulled out my diary and described what I had seen that night, and the questions that had followed. I described my unrest. I hadn't written for some days, and when I unscrewed the lid of my fountain pen, the ink spilt all over my fingers, staining them blue. A change in temperature, or something about how I had stored the pen, had caused the ink to leak into its cap. It was the most comforting thing that had happened in a long time, and I looked at my hands in relief, stained a familiar blue from writing.

There was still no reprieve, that night or the morning after, from the sensation of my heart being held in a vice. But I managed to fall asleep, and the next morn-ing I went for a walk. The pavements were wet underneath my sandals, everything clean and fresh on a summer morning. I turned things over in my mind, examining each fragment of what I had seen from different angles like a jeweller holding a faceted stone to the light, expecting fully to finally have a secret revealed. Then I tried reading my history with the two people I had seen together in light of what I had seen. The day got brighter, hotter. I sat under a tree, once again going over the same thoughts, the same questions, by this time worn smooth by my relentless attention. And then it struck me, quite simply, that I was unlikely to ever know what happened that night – all I could know was my desire for the two people I saw, and that was the only thing for which I could take any responsibility. Instead of trying to know something about the two people I had seen, I tried instead to know some-thing about my desire for them. Pulling up blades of grass as I sat underneath the tree, then tearing them up in my hand, I remembered that I wanted them, and that was the only certainty that could guide how I acted.

Although the jealousy Ernaux describes in *The Possession* is a torment, and in this it is in keeping with the associations made by Burton between melancholy and jealousy, Ernaux's depiction of jealousy also makes from the outset a link between jealousy and feelings of liveliness ('it placed me outside the grip of life's usual mediocrity'), and creative potential ('a kind of energy, powers of imagina-tion I didn't know I had') (Ernaux, 2008, p. 9). Jealousy makes something possible for Ernaux the writer. At one point Ernaux interrupts her narration of the story of her jealousy to comment upon the writing itself: 'I am writing jealousy as I lived it, tracking and accumulating the desires, sensations, and actions that were mine during this period. It's the only way for me to make something real of my obses-sion. And I am always afraid to let something essential escape. Writing, that is, as a jealousy of the real' (Ernaux, 2008, p. 34).

What does it mean, jealousy of the real? Is it that the person writing has an envious relationship with reality, hoarding its details and specificities to give to her writing, envying the variousness of the world, which her words can only index? Or does something about that phrase touch upon the way in which writing invites into itself a traumatic scene, even goes looking for it, a strategy that goes against the best wisdom of forgetting and moving on? Or is there something about writing that allows it to occupy the same space as the lack that makes jealousy both inevitable and intolerable, so that relating to the world through writing necessarily means encountering the world, first and foremost, through a lack that can't be overcome? Even in writing to possess a dispossession, which is one way of describing Ernaux's achievement in *The Possession,* there is a loss: 'it is no longer my desire, my jealousy, in these pages – it is of desire, of jealousy; I am working in invisible things' (Ernaux, 2008, p. 39).

Jealousy is often accompanied by the conviction that knowledge will be its cure, even if this knowledge is acquired in a manner that destroys the object that provoked jealousy. But there can be another way of thinking about jealousy. We can think of it as a passion for the enigma of the other's desire. To think of jealousy in this way draws attention to the foolishness of expecting that it could be solved by possessing something, either the object itself or knowledge of the object. If jealousy and its drive towards wanting and claiming to know something, somebody, in entirety, can be traversed, then it can become a form of preserving an enigma as an enigma.

In this, it shares something with a particular form of writing, which is writing as a way of having nothing, precisely because it is absence and deprivation that makes writing possible, in the most fundamental sense – an object needs to be displaced for words to take its place. And we could go further and say that the subject too needs to be displaced for words to move through her, and possess her, as writing. When Ernaux's book *The Possession* describes her possession by the other woman, it is also describing the preservation, the possession, of a loss, of a dispossession: 'Writing has been a way to save that which is no longer my reality – a sensation seizing me from head to foot, in the street – but has become "the possession", a period of time, circumscribed and completed' (Ernaux, 2008, pp. 60–61).

Writing permits, and often demands, a dispersal of the subject across its others. This is also the gift of jealousy: the subject and object of jealousy are mixed up, they are everywhere and nowhere. This movement between subject and object in writing is shared with the jealous imagination. Her jealousy makes Ernaux particularly attentive to all the women she meets, who are of a certain age, that of her lover's partner, in a 'transubstantiation of the bodies of women I encountered into the body of the other woman'. To write is also to be possessed, and to welcome such possession, to leave the doors of the house open and send its mistress into exile. The writer in these instances, far from being authoritative or self-possessed, is simply occupying a position all too familiar to the person who experiences jealousy.

On the opening page of *Simple Passion*, Ernaux describes watching 'an X rated film on Canal Plus' (Ernaux, 2022, p. 11). Then she makes the following statement: 'It occurred to me that writing should aim to do the same, to replicate the feeling of witnessing sexual intercourse, that feeling of anxiety and stupefaction, a suspension of moral judgement'. Like her other statement that writing is 'a jealousy of the real', this too is enigmatic. It brings to mind the shock and incomprehension of the primal scene, the position of exclusion to which writing is a salve, in drawing its reader into itself. When jealousy is unbearable, when it leads to something forbidden, a trespass on the other, then Anne Dufourmantelle suggests it is 'better to cultivate your own garden, invite the other to lose themselves in it, for nothing is as powerful as an invitation into yourself to heal the desire to break into the other' (Dufourmantelle, 2021, p. 104).

A few days after reckoning with my jealousy in the park, the anguish returned again, with full lurching force. This time I thought, as I have often done when confronted with something unbearable: I could try writing about this. And so it happened that when I finally set about to write about jealousy, I found myself thinking more and more about writing. I wrote the following sentence: 'writing might be a very particular form of jealousy, much as jealousy may, at times, be a form of writing to come'. I thought I would say something about how writing may soothe jealousy, using Annie Ernaux as an example, but then I noticed how my pen had betrayed me. *Writing to come* – it seemed like sexuality needed to have its due. I decided to include in the text the experience of romantic and sexual jealousy that had first created the need to write. But as I re-read the Ernaux, as I examined my experiences, I came to think that writing was no cure for jealousy, and that when I had felt myself free of jealousy, I had merely been experiencing one of its vicissitudes – writing. Like sexuality itself, and like desire, there was no resolving jealousy. And I realised that maybe that wasn't even something I wanted, after all.

At one point in *The Possession,* Ernaux writes that 'the greatest suffering, like the greatest happiness, comes from the Other' (Ernaux, 2008, p. 44). She describes the ways in which people may protect themselves from such suffering 'by loving with moderation, by favouring a match made of common interests, music, political engagement, a house with a garden etc.; or with multiple sexual partners who are seen as objects of pleasure separate from the rest of life' (Ernaux, 2008, p. 44). She uses the same word to describe her experience of jealousy that she uses at the end of *Simple Passion* regarding her love affair: Luxury. Like other luxuries, jealousy too is something to be savoured, a stroke of luck, a gift received from the plenitude of desire.

Reference list

Burton, R. (2001). *The anatomy of melancholy.* New York Review Books.

Carson, A. (2014). *The Albertine workout.* New Directions.

Dufourmantelle, A. (2021). *In defense of secrets* (L. Turner, Trans.). Fordham University Press.

Ernaux, A. (2008). *The possession* (A. Moschovakis, Trans.). Seven Stories Press.

Ernaux, A. (2022). *Simple passion* (T. Leslie, Trans.). Fitzcarraldo.

Freud, S. (2001). Mourning and melancholia. In *The standard edition of the complete works of Sigmund Freud Vol. XIV* (J. Strachey, Trans.). Vintage Books.

Chapter 7

Usurpers and rivals

Jealousy and envy in Lacan's *Family Complexes*

Kristina Valendinova

In his early 30s, Joachim was the youngest of three siblings, his brother and sister significantly older than him. In addition to being very distressed by a recent breakup, Joachim spoke of feeling stuck in his career as a graphic designer, struggling to make meaningful progress.

Joachim's relationships with his older brother Klaus had always been marked by ambivalence. During a family argument some years ago, Klaus told him that he and their sister had resented Joachim's arrival in the family, feeling that the stability their parents had finally achieved was disrupted by having to care for another child. While Joachim had tried to brush this off at the time, the impact of his brother's words stayed with him.

Joachim had looked up to Klaus as a child, but as an adult he increasingly saw him as somewhat resentful, particularly toward Joachim's creativity and artistic leanings. Klaus had pursued a career in finance but experienced multiple setbacks over the years, including a string of failed business ventures and a difficult divorce, which left him bitter and disillusioned. In their interactions, Klaus often took on a patronising tone, giving Joachim unsolicited advice on everything from his professional choices to his fitness regime. When Joachim's relationship ended, Klaus initially seemed supportive, encouraging his brother to 'move on' and even suggesting people for him to date, but also eager to tell Joachim every time he ran into his ex-boyfriend in town.

While Joachim was grateful, these interventions often left him feeling undermined and frustrated, as if his brother's input was more about asserting his own superiority. In therapy, he reflected on how his brother's life had fallen short of his family's expectations. Deep down, Joachim had always feared that he too would fail to meet their parents' high standards and, despite his talents and hard work, would end up like Klaus – creatively and emotionally unfulfilled. He was torn between his anger at his brother's interference and a deep sense of guilt, which Klaus's envy only intensified: contrary to his brother's highly critical views on their family and childhood, Joachim's later arrival meant that he had experienced their parents as much more present and supportive than his older siblings had.

Outside his family, Joachim's life had also been marked by a fear of provoking envy in others. Reflecting on his school years, he described his difficulties in

DOI: 10.4324/9781032637549-7

making friends, feeling that his peers were jealous of his family's comfortable lifestyle or his cultural interests. This interpretation had been encouraged by his mother, who often warned him against wanting to stand out too much. In his current career, which required a great deal of initiative and self-promotion, Joachim struggled to make himself visible or take credit for his work, fearing it would once again stir resentment or dislike. Despite his talent and hard work, his reluctance to compete left him overshadowed by less capable colleagues. His own feelings of envy and jealousy towards more successful peers were equally difficult to confront: it was as though admitting to such emotions would make them spiral out of control.

Joachim was thus left with very little room for manoeuvre: seeking recognition always meant provoking envy, and therefore guilt, while holding back meant he was failing to fulfil his family's aspirations, as well as his own potential. There seemed to be no way to navigate these conflicting emotions, leaving him perpetually questioning his own worth and purpose.

Jealousy, including envy and rivalry among siblings, has been among the earliest topics of psychoanalytic interest. Perhaps no other emotion has been so likened to a physical disease, a corrosive condition slowly consuming the patient from within. No wonder that in many European languages, one is said to 'go green' or 'be green' with jealousy. This connects with the ancient theory of the body's four humours, where the colour green signified an excess of yellow bile, associated with the choleric (from the Greek *chole* for bile) temperament: irritable, suspicious, and easily provoked. For psychoanalysis, jealousy is both a banal, universal emotion and a manifestation of psychic conflict, with roots running deep into childhood – according to those influenced by the work of Melanie Klein, even into earliest infancy. Despite the persistent stirrings of envy through today's social media, it remains an emotion that is difficult to accept in both ourselves and others. Parents of young children often go to great lengths to avoid accusations of 'preferential treatment', and despite the number of books written on sibling rivalry, many still struggle to watch their offspring fight each other with the intensity of determined little warriors, ignoring the adults' desperate pleas to 'share'.

In this chapter, I explore the complexities of sibling jealousy and its connections to sociality and the genesis of social feelings – a link recognised by both Freud and Lacan, who understood the dual nature of jealousy as destructive and constructive. In his paper on *Family Complexes*, Lacan transforms sibling rivalry into the concept of an 'intrusion complex'. While this concept disappears from his theory, it nonetheless articulates many of his later ideas on the genesis of the human psyche and provides insight into how to approach the dialectic of jealousy and its excesses. I am particularly interested in the various vectors of jealousy. While we usually think of jealousy and envy as one-sided afflictions of the jealous person alone, what is it like from the other side? What is it like to be the object of envy, or even to provoke it? And, as we have seen in Joachim's case, how might this shape one's later conduct and identifications?

An intimate friend, a hated enemy

In his letter to Fliess from October 3, 1897, Freud lists a few fresh discoveries from his ongoing self-analysis, including his 'genuine childhood jealousy' (Freud, 1950, p. 264) of his one-year-younger brother Julius, who died as an infant after only a few months, his death leaving Sigmund with 'the germ of self-reproaches in me' (Freud, 1950). As we know, Freud was the oldest child of his father's third marriage; he had two much older half-brothers, and after Julius's death, when Sigmund was 11 months old, five more siblings followed, meaning that his young mother was constantly preoccupied with new babies. He also had two companions of similar age, his niece Pauline and especially his nephew John: 'Until the end of my third year, we had been inseparable. We had loved each other and fought with each other; and this childhood relationship . . . had a determining influence on all my subsequent relations with contemporaries' (1900, p. 424). The two children left for England when Sigmund was three. The loss of this relationship is apparent to Freud: 'All my friends have in a certain sense been reincarnations of this first figure who [". . . long since appeared before my troubled gaze"]: they have been *revenants*' (1900, p. 483). Commenting on the ambivalence of this initial relationship, Freud was aware of its having informed a pattern of friendships that would repeat throughout his life and career:

> My emotional life has always insisted that I should have an intimate friend and a hated enemy. I have always been able to provide myself afresh with both, and it has not infrequently happened that the ideal situation of childhood has been so completely reproduced that friend and enemy have come together in a single individual.
>
> (1900, p. 483)

Prior to Wilhelm Fliess, there had been Eduard Silberstein, with whom Freud maintained intense correspondence throughout his teenage years, and of course, Breuer, Adler, Jung, Ferenczi, where we see the same progression from idealisation to hostility.

In *The Interpretation of Dreams*, a work largely based on Freud's self-analysis, he writes that observing the behaviour of small children up to the age of two or three towards their younger sibling makes it clear that the elder child is rarely pleased with the new arrival, and even if he 'only comes to realise the situation later on, his hostility will date from that moment . . . Children at that time of life are capable of "jealousy" of any degree of intensity and obviousness' (1900, p. 251). If the new baby should disappear, as was the case with Freud's younger brother, the older child will be able to reclaim the total affection of the parents, but if another one comes along, it's logical that one might wish for it to meet the same fate. These deaths might be forgotten but have a very important influence on subsequent neuroses. 'Hostile feelings towards brothers and sisters must be far more frequent in childhood than the unseeing eye of the adult observer can perceive', Freud writes (p. 252). And also:

I do not know why we presuppose that that relation must be a loving one; for instances of hostility between adult brothers and sisters force themselves upon everyone's experience and we can often establish the fact that the disunity originated in childhood or has always existed. But it is further true that a great many adults, who are on affectionate terms with their brothers and sisters and are ready to stand by them to-day, passed their childhood on almost unbroken terms of enmity with them. The elder child ill-treats the younger, maligns him and robs him of his toys; while the younger is consumed with impotent rage against the elder, envies and fears him, or meets his oppressor with the first stirrings of a love of liberty and a sense of justice.

(1900, p. 250)

From the beginning of his theoretical journey, the unwelcome arrival of a sibling therefore figures prominently as a major event of childhood, confronting the child not just with the pain and disillusionment of having to share the caregivers' love and attention, but also with the burning questions of how babies come about, as well as sexual difference. In the study of Little Hans, the boy is jealous of his new sister, commenting on her lack of teeth, but also intrigued and troubled by her small 'widdler', which he optimistically expects to grow.

In all cases, Freud is therefore sensitive to the complexity of sibling rivalry: while the painful experience leaves a permanent mark (guilt), allowing old jealousies to be stirred again in adult age, including in the relationship with the analyst, the new sibling is also someone new to love – and occasionally terrorise – allowing the older child to move towards new ventures and explorations. In *Some Neurotic Mechanisms in Jealousy, Paranoia and Homosexuality* (1922), Freud distinguishes between three levels of jealousy: first, the normal painful feelings caused by the fear of losing the loved object and enmity towards more successful rivals; second, projected jealousy, which is the subject's own guilt due to actual or potential unfaithfulness, projected onto others. This second type is amenable to analytic work. The third type, delusional jealousy, is not, since its object is of the same sex as the subject, and the latter defends themselves against this forbidden desire by a more radical measure, projecting it onto another person, following the formula Freud identifies as *I (a man) do not love him; she loves him!* What was abolished internally therefore comes back from the outside.

Freud observes this peculiarity of jealousy, its two poles: a basic childhood experience that most of us are forced to learn to tolerate, even when it resurges in later life, and which in fact universally leads to the birth of the individual's social instincts; versus the pathological excesses we find in certain conditions. Just as a degree of 'normal' jealousy goes hand in hand with any experience of love we fear to lose, most of the hostile and destructive impulses towards our childhood rivals have to be transformed into tenderness and, on a larger social scale, the affectionate and social feelings of identification which situate us as members of our various tribes. In *The Ego and the Id*, Freud writes that the most mundane social feelings are thus a superstructure built on the hellfire of infantile jealousies against our brothers and sisters (Freud, 1923, p. 37). As he specifies towards the end of his life in *New Introductory Lectures*:

> All of this has been very long familiar and is accepted as self-evident; but we rarely form a correct idea of the strength of these jealous impulses, of the tenacity with which they persist and of the magnitude of their influence on later development. Especially as this jealousy is constantly receiving fresh nourishment in the later years of childhood and the whole shock is repeated with the birth of each new brother or sister. Nor does it make much difference if the child happens to remain the mother's preferred favourite. A child's demands for love are immoderate, they make exclusive claims and tolerate no sharing.
>
> (Freud, 1933, p. 123)

The usurper

It is this contrast between the immoderate demands of the infantile unconscious and their translation into the fabric of our societies that Lacan tries to address in his paper on the *Family Complexes* (Lacan, 1938). As Lacan was a young psychiatrist not yet influenced by linguistics or structuralism, the paper makes no mention of the signifier, the three orders of human experience, object a, or the Name-of-the-Father – though all of these can be found in potentia. For example, his use of the terms 'cultural' or 'socio-cultural' and his emphasis on 'communication' suggest the later concept of the symbolic, particularly in his careful focus on the relative autonomy of human development from certain biological realities.

The very idea of the complex itself anticipates a more structural reading: originally coined by the Zurich psychoanalytic school, a complex refers to a set of ideas and memories with strong affective value – a relatively stable arrangement that remains unconscious, while its individual elements can be brought into consciousness. Freud himself really spoke of only two complexes – the Oedipus complex and the castration complex[1] – but Lacan adopts and generalises the term to distinguish it from the concept of instinct as a biological force. A complex is not entirely unrelated to biology, such as the fundamental prematurity of human infants, but it is culturally determined and transmitted, binding the instincts into a stable form. It reflects the psychic reality of a particular developmental stage and can later be reactivated when certain experiences occur. Rather than serving as vital functions, complexes use cultural means to compensate for human functional deficiencies in the face of biological existence. In what might seem like an uncharacteristically developmental text for Lacan, the three complexes presented here (the weaning complex, the fraternal complex, and the Oedipus complex) are logical rather than chronological points in a series governed by retroaction, where each point both anticipates and reactivates the others.

Thus, there is nothing 'natural' about weaning, which, as a cultural practice, takes many forms – just consider the ever-changing attitudes towards breastfeeding.

That does not make it any less of a trauma, leaving a permanent trace on the psyche in the form of an unconscious 'imago' of wholeness – a quasi-symbiotic, nurturing relationship that has been interrupted and lost, which the subject forever struggles to restore. While there is, of course, an actual physical – and dramatic – separation of the child from the mother's body at birth, and though the child may experience distress even prior to birth, it is weaning that provides these feelings with a more precise psychic form. Interestingly, Lacan also believes this process underpins the mother's own 'motherly' feelings. In this view, mothering is, among many other things, a compensation, a complex rather than an instinct, and the mother's translation of this early separation influences her conduct to 'protect the child from an abandonment that would be fatal to them' (Lacan, 1938, p. 34). No wonder, then, that Lacan later says that weaning is a trauma primarily for mothers!

On the whole, the child either accepts or refuses this separation, but what is the nature of this choice, given that there is no ego? At best, it is ambivalent. At this time, Lacan doesn't yet speak about symbolisation of this loss; he argues that weaning must be sublimated, pushing the child towards new relationships in the world beyond the mother. However, 'the maternal imago possesses the very depths of the psyche' (Lacan, 1938, p. 35),[2] making this process particularly difficult. As much as it resists sublimation, the maternal imago becomes a factor of death (Lacan, 1938).[3]

Against the background of this first loss, Lacan now introduces what is ultimately a short-lived theoretical construction: the intrusion complex, or fraternal complex. After making a brief appearance in several of Lacan's early writings – his dissertation on the case of Aimée, his commentary on the crime of the Papin sisters – the concept is eventually abandoned in favour of the mirror stage, where the genesis of the ego becomes more explicitly Freudian. However, the intrusion complex provides a way of understanding jealousy and its excesses through the lens of Lacan's later distinction between the imaginary and the symbolic axes of human experience, offering an alternative reading of what Freud had already identified as the intricate relationship between jealousy, normalcy, and pathology.

In this paper, Lacan 'inserts' the intrusion complex prior to the Oedipus complex, framing it as a situation in which we first experience envy, while simultaneously situating ourselves as social beings – similar to others, but also in tension with them. This adds a horizontal axis to the vertical relationship between us and our primary caregivers, addressing not just jealousy and envy but the ambivalence between love and identification, between similarity and difference.

In this scenario we perceive ourselves as lacking, as having lost something the other still possesses or could potentially have. For the first time, Lacan quotes a scene from Augustine's *Confessions*, to which he repeatedly returns in his seminars. In this passage, Augustine observes a small child jealous of his nursing baby brother: 'I have myself seen jealousy in a baby and know what it means. He was not old enough to talk, but, whenever he saw his foster-brother at the breast, he would grow pale with envy'. From this, Lacan concludes that the aggressiveness inherent in jealousy is, in fact, secondary:

> In delineating the structure of infant jealousy, experimental observations of the child as well as psychoanalytic investigations reveal its role in the genesis of sociability and, through that, of human consciousness itself. The critical point discovered by these projects is that jealousy, in its fundamental form, represents not so much a deep-seated rivalry as a mental identification.
>
> (Lacan, 1938, p. 37)

Lacan points out that in this situation, the object of envy (the breast, the feeding) cannot be understood as a 'vital' object of competition. Presumably the older child was also fed and, having been weaned, no longer needs maternal milk. Something else is at stake here – an image of enjoyment from which the older child has already been excluded, reactivating the maternal imago left behind by the experience of weaning. This is what enables Lacan to argue that jealousy is never justified by its object. It is not a vital competition, a fundamental struggle for scarce resources; its object is not one of need but, as he would later describe it, of enjoyment. Thus, 'human jealousy distinguishes itself in this way from basic survival competition since it creates its object instead of discovering it' (Lacan, 1938, p. 43). An object becomes worth desiring, worth our attention, only as far as it is desired by another, which the ego takes as its model. Similarly, the object created is one that is always already lost. The rival is perceived as still inhabiting the primordial state of abundance, not yet ejected from it.

He continues to say that jealousy is thus 'the archetype of all social feelings' (Lacan, 1938). The shocking intrusion of this usurper establishes the kind of relationship Lacan later refers to as imaginary: a dynamic marked by both captivation and fascination with the other, but also a mutual exclusion: the child perceives the situation as a choice between themselves or the rival – it's him or me! Crucially, this provides a solution to the inchoate anxieties of the previous complex. As mentioned earlier, the child both accepts and rejects weaning, but for a dialectic to be established, the image of the rival serves to solidify the 'negative' pole of this ambivalence, externalising the internal conflict.

In the remainder of this section, Lacan revisits the mirror stage, which corresponds to this type of identification. Similar to the situation with the nursing brother, the mirror image, which the infant reacts to with jubilation, is highly charged. It reactivates the image of wholeness against the backdrop of the child's bodily experience, marked by fragmentation. This type of identification with the rival reinforces both competition and alienation: 'Before the ego affirms its identity, it is confused with this image which not only forms it but also profoundly alienates it' (Lacan, 1938). This identification is crucial in developing sociality, as it introduces the subject into the field of others, creating relations of rivalry over objects of desire. However, to navigate these relationships, another step is required: the imaginary rivalry must evolve into a symbolic competition where subjects can take up and lose positions within the symbolic structure.

Lacan's paper is undoubtedly influenced, in part, by Klein's work on envy, although the latter is too complex to summarise here. Klein's later distinction (which Lacan does not explicitly make) between envy and jealousy is, however, relevant: envy seeks to spoil or destroy the desirable object that one's rival possesses, and it harks back to the exclusivity between the child and the mother (Klein, 1957). Jealousy, on the other hand, involves the fear of losing love and requires a triangular structure. We could say that where envy simply wants to destroy the object, jealousy seeks to assert oneself over one's rival. The word 'envy' comes from the Latin *invidere*, meaning 'to look upon with malice', akin to the 'evil eye' – a look that seeks to harm but also harms the subject, as seen in the deadly pallor of Augustine's envious observer. For Klein, envy is the more primitive emotion, while jealousy belongs specifically to the oedipal stage. This aligns with Lacan's comments here: the fraternal complex serves as a transitional stage from envy to jealousy, from an imaginary identification to what will later become a symbolic one. In Lacan's paper, the sequence of the complexes functions to translate the child's primitive anxieties through a series of stages.[4]

The Oedipus complex, which for Lacan coincides with the peak of the child's genital drives (a kind of psychological puberty), introduces a new element: attributing the frustration of the child's oedipal desires to the father. However, contrary to Freud's view of the father as the agent of castration, for Lacan this is merely a fantasy that generates a new defence against the primitive anxieties, which had been only imperfectly bound by the previous imagos. The fraternal complex, centred on identification through rivalry, provided the child with an image of unity to identify with, but this identification remained alienating, underpinned by an anxiety of fragmentation. The Oedipus complex, driven by jealousy towards the father, further stabilises the imaginary field through a new fixed point of reference: the paternal imago.

Contrary to the maternal imago, which represents a point of negativity within the psyche, binding archaic anxieties, this new agency both represses sexual desire through the fear of castration and results in the creation of the ego-ideal, offering the subject new avenues of sublimation. These allow the child to form relationships where rivalry and hatred are pacified, made bearable through love and tenderness. The child can now see himself not merely in competition with his siblings but as part of a larger family dynamic, where different members occupy different places and responsibilities, and where one can aspire to be loved by espousing the family's values, taking on symbolic roles rooted in the acceptance of difference.

At this time, Lacan's notion of Oedipus conflict underscores the ways in which the imaginary identification with the rival (a sibling, a child of similar age), marked by feelings of envy and aggressiveness, is transformed into a more robust sense of social subjecthood by the child identifying with an ideal image. In his later work, this ideal image is upheld by language and the symbolic fabric of human society, but already in this paper, we see that the 'paternal imago' represents a qualitative leap with respect to the previous two imagoes. Crucially, this movement superimposes the latter type of identification over the former, replacing imaginary envy with the symbolic play of jealousy in the oedipal framework, forming the basis for the child's broader socialisation.

Family transmissions

In terms of how this journey is made for each child, Lacan emphasises the role of cultural factors and contingencies, such as the children's age difference and their place in the family 'dynasty'. In working clinically with children, the arrival of a new baby is of course a major event, and sibling rivalry manifests in a myriad of ways: sometimes as open hostility, or more silently through regressive symptoms (e.g. bedwetting, sleep disturbances, loss of language or other skills). These reactions, often trivialised or ignored by parents, interact with other family dynamics, particularly the parents' own relationship. Contrary to popular theories of birth order which simply assign set personality traits to specific positions (cf. the endless stream of TikTok videos on 'eldest daughter syndrome'), the signifiers that determine a child's place in the family are carried across generations, and often the unsaid has the greatest influence. In this context, it is important to note that parental perceptions of sibling dynamics, including envy, jealousy, and favouritism, are shaped by how similar experiences have been inscribed in the parents' own unconscious.

Linh sought therapy for anxiety and body image issues, but she also disclosed a habit of bingeing and purging, particularly during moments of high stress. Since puberty, she had struggled with her weight; although she tried endless diets, even when they occasionally worked, her self-perception hardly improved. Linh avoided having her picture taken, and even accidentally seeing her reflection would trigger a flood of intense self-criticism. The bingeing and purging provided temporary relief but also frightened her due to its violent nature, further increasing her anxiety about her appearance.

Linh's family had fled their home country due to political unrest. As a well-connected family, they quickly established themselves in their new country, though they remained closely tied to their roots, vigilantly following the political situation back home. Linh's mother, who had been left behind by her own mother to be raised by aunts, had a complicated relationship with her siblings. After Linh's birth, her parents' marriage grew fractious: Linh's father was frequently away on business, and in his absence, her mother would confide in Linh but also take out her frustrations on her, sometimes beating her and calling her a disappointment. Despite this, Linh held a special place amongst her cousins as her grandmother's favourite and even after her grandmother's death continued to be praised as the most dutiful grandchild. She was often asked to mediate in family disputes, a responsibility that felt overwhelming yet impossible to escape.

At the start of therapy, Linh described herself as a 'burden' on others. Growing up, she had felt a constant pressure to be perfect. In her family, appearances mattered, and failure was seen as a personal flaw. Women of her social class were expected to be confident, polished, and, above all, thin. Linh's weight was a frequent topic of conversation, with relatives freely commenting and offering advice as if her body was not her own but a reflection of the family's collective reputation.

Socially, Linh devoted significant energy to counselling and supporting her less accomplished friends. However, when she attempted to share her own fears and insecurities with them, it often backfired. Her family typically responded by telling her that others were simply envious of her success. Their jealousy was seen as normal and expected – a sign of the family's prestige. Yet for Linh, these painful experiences confirmed that any deviation from her 'perfect image' unsettled those around her, driving her continuous strive for self-improvement, while also leaving her isolated and questioning whether she could ever form genuine connections.

Linh's self-doubt was continually reinforced by her family's mixed messages: was she the ideal, dutiful daughter, or a disappointment, failing to meet their expectations? She struggled to relinquish the impossible standards that loyalty to her family compelled her to embody – standards that never seemed to win her favour among ordinary people. Her inner conflict manifested in her preoccupation with her physical appearance, as well as her bingeing and purging – compulsive attempts to alleviate the pressure.

Jealousy and paranoia

The second part of Lacan's paper on the complexes is concerned with the relationship between the developmental model he has introduced and its failures, leading to different pathologies, both neurotic and psychotic. As we have seen, the complexes translate a certain reality of the subject's environment and gradually produce a communicable relationship with the world of others. Already in this early model, we observe that subjectivity and the apparent unity of the body image must be produced and arrived at, rather than being a given. Akin to Freud's idea of fixation points, alongside this process, there are various points of complication. The stakes are high, as evidenced when Lacan writes about the fraternal complex, explaining that the subject has to make a choice. The ego is constituted simultaneously with the other. In this 'drama of jealousy', the emergence of a third object introduces competition and, with it, the subject

> enters into a new alternative where *the fate of reality is at stake*: either he finds the maternal object again and clings to the refusal of reality and the destruction of the other; or, led to some other object, he receives it in the characteristic form of human knowledge, as a communicable object, since competition implies both rivalry and agreement; but at the same time, he recognizes the other with whom the struggle or contract is engaged, in short, he finds both the other and the socialised object.
>
> (Lacan, 1938, p. 43, my emphasis)

In the opposite case, paranoia is one of the conditions linked to the failure of recognition:

> The connections between paranoia and the fraternal complex are manifested by the frequent themes of filiation, usurpation, and dispossession, just as its narcissistic structure is revealed in more paranoid themes of intrusion, influence, duplication, the double, and all the delusional transmutations of the body.
>
> (Lacan, 1938, p. 45)

Freud had long noted the connection between jealousy and paranoia, culminating in his 1922 paper, where he distinguished between 'normal' jealousy and its more pathological forms in paranoia, namely the delusional projection of jealousy onto a person of the same sex. In 1932, the same year in which he defended his dissertation on the case of 'Aimée' (dedicated to his younger brother), Lacan translated Freud's text into French as his first contribution to psychoanalytic scholarship.

Marguerite Pantain-Anzieu, whom Lacan nicknamed Aimée, was arrested in 1930 after attempting to stab the actress Huguette Duflos, whom she believed had been threatening Marguerite's young son. Marguerite, a sensitive child from a peasant family, had always considered herself exceptional. However, as a young woman, her professional and romantic aspirations were repeatedly thwarted. After marrying a coworker, her first breakdown occurred during her pregnancy when her older sister Élise moved in with the couple and took over the household duties. Élise's domineering and critical presence deepened Marguerite's sense of failure and isolation, eventually escalating into delusions of surveillance, along with a growing sense of threat to herself and her baby, who was later delivered stillborn. Though Marguerite delivered a healthy child in her second pregnancy, her mental state continued to deteriorate. She became convinced that she was destined to become a novelist and social reformer and moved to Paris, leaving her son in Élise's care. However, these ambitions constantly failed, and as her isolation deepened, Marguerite developed an intricate delusional system, which included erotomaniac themes, but was mostly centred on a belief that her artistic and professional failures resulted from a conspiracy involving several public figures, namely Duflos, who plagiarised her own writings but, crucially, also posed an acute threat to her son's life.

Lacan's analysis highlighted the unusual fact that Marguerite's delusions vanished entirely not immediately after the stabbing, but several weeks after her arrest. This led him to coin the term 'self-punishing paranoia' (Lacan, 1932, p. 268), a delusional condition rooted in Marguerite's unconscious guilt. He also noticed the repetition of same-sex persecutors, which he related to Freud's analysis of Schreber. Alongside a string of famous actresses and intellectuals (Sarah Bernhardt, Colette, etc.), whose corruption Marguerite decries in her writings, these also included Mlle C – a wealthy socialite Marguerite befriended as a single woman, whose phone call just after the first baby's death marked her as the first persecutor. All these figures represent enviable, powerful, and glamorous women – embodying an ideal Marguerite could never reach.

At first glance, it may seem that Marguerite is simply striking out in envy at those she wished to become. However, according to Lacan, the prototype of these persecutors is, in fact, her older sister Élise, whom Lacan, after interviewing her, described in highly unflattering terms. Élise's primary concern during their meeting was ensuring that Marguerite remained institutionalised. In Lacan's view, Élise was the true 'usurper', having taken over Marguerite's roles as mother and de facto wife. Élise justified her control by citing Marguerite's supposed inexperience, despite the fact that, as their family had attested, Marguerite had been providing perfectly adequate care for her child, and her mental state had improved whenever she resumed those duties. Lacan believed that, despite Élise's domineering and critical attitude, Marguerite could not confront her directly – not just due to a lack of support, but because she consciously acknowledged Élise's qualities, having been raised by her as a young child. 'The familial nature of the bond that unites her with her most intimate enemy helps to explain the systematic misrecognition where Aimée seeks refuge' (p. 233).

Thus, the patient's delusion functions as a defence against this unresolvable conflict, displacing it onto a series of idealised persecutors. Unlike Élise, these women – largely interchangeable and of purely symbolic value – are not protected from Marguerite's anger. 'She substitutes the object directly offered to her hatred with another object that has provoked similar reactions in her . . . but which has the advantage of being out of reach of her blows' (p. 234). The recurring theme of being deprived of her child or the threat to the child's life runs through these delusions, revealing the core unresolved conflict.

Lacan's reading of the case inverts the manifest vector of envy: it is not Marguerite who is striking out at others' enjoyment, but rather Élise – childless, widowed, and hysterectomised – who robs her of her rightful place as a mother and wife. Marguerite's sensitive disposition, along with her prior attachment to and admiration for her older sister, left her unable to defend herself, triggering the delusion. In this way, an older sibling successfully usurps the younger's place, driving her toward madness, and Lacan's interpretation intervenes as a rectification of this narrative.

In the 1990s psychoanalyst Jean Allouch (1997) revisited the case after one of Lacan's patients, Didier Anzieu, abruptly ended his analysis with Lacan upon revealing he was Marguerite's son. Allouch's reading sheds additional light on certain aspects of the family history that Lacan's version had insufficiently addressed. Some years before Marguerite's birth, her mother's first child, also named Marguerite, tragically died in an accident, burning to death at the family home at the age of five. The accident was witnessed by her two younger siblings, including the three-year-old Élise, while their mother Jeanne was likely absent. Another pregnancy followed, resulting in a stillborn child, after which Jeanne gave birth to 'our' Marguerite, who was subsequently placed in Élise's care as Jeanne's mental state deteriorated into what the family described as 'persecutory madness'. Jeanne, who was still alive (and experiencing another episode) at the time of Marguerite's arrest, is conspicuously absent from Lacan's account, possibly due to the family's efforts to shield her from further distress.

The repetition of child deaths and the interchangeability of names suggest a profound confusion of symbolic positions within the family. Additionally, there is continuity between Jeanne's and Marguerite's delusions, both of which attribute the blame for a child's death to another person. For Allouch, it is not Élise but rather the 'original' Marguerite – or indeed, her tragic death – who exerts a persecutory force on the later Marguerite's life. Allouch's intricate reading of the Pantain family history and the recurrence of female psychosis focuses on Lacan's later concept of the foreclosure of the non-existence of the sexual relationship. Marguerite's triggering during her pregnancies relates to the impossibility of subjectivising her position as a sexed subject, with the child as a – threatening and therefore threatened – revelation of her sexuality. The election of her persecutors, as women she perceives as openly expressive of their sexuality, reflects this foreclosure. What Marguerite sees in the actress she attacks is thus not merely an ideal of empowered femininity, nor simply a figure attempting to rob her of her child, but a distorted, mocking image of female sexuality – one that is tainted, demeaning, and corrupted, yet also corrupts in turn: the figure of the whore.

However, Allouch also interrogates Lacan's transference to his patient, which led him to enthusiastically adopt the role of her 'secretary' (Allouch, 1997, p. 420): he published her writings and poems in his thesis (this was met with some consternation by his teachers, and also, Lacan never returned Marguerite's writings, despite her requests), but also secured her a job in the hospital library and intervened in her family relationships. Specifically, regarding Marguerite's older sister, his attitude could indeed be seen as a form of rivalry (it was either her or him!). This is evident both in his designation of Élise as the 'usurper' in his interpretation of the case and in his assertiveness in deciding on Marguerite's care. While Élise urged Marguerite to abandon her lofty literary ambitions, Lacan, on the contrary, encouraged them, treating her writings as a valuable source of insight. He also sought to theoretically elaborate on a mode of thought specific to paranoia, viewing delusions not merely as deficient productions but, following Freud, as an 'interpretative activity of the unconscious' (Lacan, 1932, p. 293).

Their encounter was decisive, leading Lacan to pivot towards Freudian psychoanalysis. As Elisabeth Roudinesco tells us, he began his treatment with Rudolph Lowenstein in 1932, just as he was finishing his interviews with Marguerite (Roudinesco, 1997, p. 69). The material from the Aimée case and its interpretation, which underscores the element of sibling rivalry, reverberates through Lacan's early theoretical writings, including the first paper on the *Mirror Stage* and the 1938 paper on the *Family Complexes*. The centrality of the sibling relationship as a prototype of sociality prefigures his later ideas on the genesis of the ego, the body image, and the distinction between neurosis and psychosis.

In this chapter, I have used clinical examples to show that the vectors of envy and jealousy are complex and the specific coordinates which determine on which side the different subjects find themselves are typically transmitted across generations. However, Lacan's theory also shows that beyond the individual struggles for parental love and attention, experiences of envy and jealousy are also pivotal moments in the subject's entry into social life. His assertion that 'jealousy is the archetype of all social feelings' (Lacan, 1938, p. 43) encapsulates this dual function of jealousy recognised by psychoanalysis: both destructive, driving aggressiveness and hostility, and constructive, pushing the subject towards socialisation and the recognition of difference.

Notes

1 While Freud remained critical of the term's apparent popularity, decrying it as a 'Jungian complex-mythology', psychoanalysis has indeed had an appetite for complexes: the father complex, masculinity and femininity complex, loss complex, anal complex, sibling complex, menstruation complex, and of course the many named after mythological characters: the Medea complex, the Demosthenes complex, the Icarus, the Jocasta, the Laius and Ulysses, the Oresteia, the Asclepius, the Orpheus, the Achilles, and, of course, the Electra complex.
2 This imago also appears in the forms of images of dwellings and thresholds, in humanity's utopian longings for the paradise lost, etc.
3 In the clinic, he writes, we see this connection between the death drive and the maternal in the 'non-violent' suicides where the subject gives up on life in order to regain the maternal imago; for instance, the hunger strike of anorexia, drug addictions (self-poisoning), and the starvation diets of the gastric neuroses.
4 In 1951, when Lacan returned to the topic in his paper presented to the British Psychoanalytic Society, *Some Reflections on the Ego*, in which he was trying to introduce his Mirror State to the English analysts. Alongside many of the elements contained in his earlier paper on the mirror stage (e.g., the role mimetism plays in the development of certain species, the question of transitivism), we find many more references to Klein's work, including the more careful distinction between envy and jealousy.

Reference list

Allouch, J. (1997). *Marguerite ou l'Aimée de Lacan*. EPEL.
Freud, S. (1950). Letter to Fliess, October 3, 1897. In *Standard edition* (Vol. 1, p. 264). Hogarth Press.
Freud, S. (1953). The interpretation of dreams. In *Standard edition* (Vols. 4–5). The Hogarth Press (Original work published 1900).
Freud, S. (1955). Some neurotic mechanisms in jealousy, paranoia and homosexuality. In *Standard edition* (Vol. 18, pp. 221–232). The Hogarth Press (Original work published 1922).
Freud, S. (1961). The ego and the id. In *Standard edition* (Vol. 19, pp. 1–66). The Hogarth Press. (Original work published 1923)
Freud, S. (1964). New introductory lectures on psychoanalysis. In *Standard edition* (Vol. 22, pp. 1–182). The Hogarth Press (Original work published 1933).
Klein, M. (1957). *Envy and gratitude: A study of unconscious sources*. Tavistock.
Lacan, J. (1932). *De la psychose paranoïaque dans ses rapports avec la personnalité*. Le François.
Lacan, J. (1977). The mirror stage as formative of the i function as revealed in psychoanalytic experience. In A. Sheridan (Trans.), *Écrits: A selection*. W.W. Norton & Company. (Original work published 1949)
Lacan, J. (1993). *The seminar of Jacques Lacan, book III: The psychoses 1955–1956* (J.-A. Miller, Ed., & R. Grigg, Trans.). W.W. Norton & Company.
Lacan, J. (2001). Les complexes familiaux dans la formation de l'individu. In J.-A. Miller (Ed.), *Autres Écrits* (pp. 23–84). Seuil (Original work published 1938).
Roudinesco, E. (1997). *Jacques Lacan* (B. Bray, Trans.). Columbia University Press.

Chapter 8

Jealousy

Gazes, mothers, America

Jamieson Webster

The gaze as demand for the mother

In today's social media–dominated world, the gaze has new traction and reach for subjects. While this seems like a such a commonplace observation (why even say it?), this infinite gazing is a new source of merciless super-egoic interrogation that mocks all genuine psychoanalytic inquiry. I sometimes now feel I must pretend not to look at a thing, for fear of awakening this monstrous eye. The analyst who used to have to say very little, must now see very little too. But what is being looked at? Or what is this looking propping up?

We envy what we see of another person's life and enjoyment that we know nothing of. The picture seems to say it all, when in fact it says very little. The process that the image sets in motion requires that we remain vigilant of what we think we have seen, as if to seal it there in the totality we have witnessed. More meaning, or less meaning, would threaten this fragile psyche by re-opening a question of what was looked at or seen. Indeed, opening a question of whether any such totality can be found; and what this has to do with us, no less our desire.

So much of our experience remains unconscious – a place absolutely embodied – a repression reinforced by disembodied looking and thinking. It now seems to me that the reach of the gaze moves in the direction of maintaining this frozenness of looking and withdrawal into oneself. Divine vision, which included any mistakes and all future events, has been transferred to the subject and their gaze. The future isn't one of redemption, promise, or condemnation, but it is deferred as an immediate infinity. Even the affect of envy, no doubt omnipresent, feels deferred.

Freud commented often on the human's upright posture and exaggerated reliance on sight in comparison to the sensory world of animals. While smell tells you exactly what you need to know as an animal, sight, in fact, often tells you very little – it is fraught with misunderstanding. We often don't know what we are looking at. Freud thus holds unconscious desire up against the gaze. The gaze is a powerful source of illusion, especially of our separateness and supposed individual sovereignty.

Lacan was the first to really theorise the splitting of the gaze following Freud as a phenomenologically palpable version of the Freudian split subject. As he says

DOI: 10.4324/9781032637549-8

beautifully, 'you never look at me from the place that I see you. Conversely, what I look at is never what I wish to see' (Lacan Seminar XI, p. 103) Lacan goes into great detail on Freud's 'Father, can't you see that I'm burning' dream. The phrase was uttered to the dreamer by his child, who had just died of fever. But the dead child also caught fire when a candle fell on his shrouded body – the father having fallen asleep during his vigil. The fire outside entered the dream so the father could continue to sleep in order to see his child one last time. But which reality is worse, Lacan asks – the one inside the dream, or the one outside? The candle that falls, or falling asleep?

The invocation of the gaze – father, can't you see – sets off the problem. See what? See what is no longer visible? But that's the last thing we want to see. As the philosopher Merleau-Ponty notes, seeing abhors a vacuum. Nothing is worse than never seeing your child again, but what this father sees in trying to see him a final time is not only the horror of death, his child burning, but a depth of guilt in the form of vicious, recriminating words. Look at me! You were asleep. You let me burn. This is precisely what looking wants to avoid, having to remain frozen, caught at a threshold of any Real encounter, keeping itself close to its own demand.

Certainly, the gaze always encounters something from which one is excluded. But what we are excluded from, how we are excluded, and even if we are excluded, are difficult questions to wrestle with. This is one way of thinking of the gaze and the image as a process of closure. Simply that, the encounter with a closure. Lacan tells another story about the gaze along these lines.

Reminiscing about a moment from his 20s, he says he wanted to experience something more real, something gritty, physical, dangerous. So he goes out with some fisherman in Brittany, a place, he remarks, that is not industrialised, meaning it is a job at their own risk, a different kind of exploitation to that of industry. He is at sea with these fisherman, waiting to pull in the nets, and they happen upon a sardine can floating at sea. This object is like a visitor from the commercial future that will render their current way of life obsolete.

The can is glittering in the sunlight and a fisherman, clearly amused, says to Lacan, 'You see that can? Well, it doesn't see you!' Lacan notes that the sardine can *is* in fact looking at him. It is the point of light, the line of sight, that shows the picture that he is in. The picture is a picture where these fisherman laugh at this boy who is out of place, has no real reason to be there. This is why he couldn't find the joke funny.

The picture is in our eye, Lacan states, but we do not see ourselves in it. Yet, we constantly show ourselves to the gaze of the other, meaning we live within the frame of the Other's looking at us. There is no overlap between this split. The philosopher Merleau-Ponty, on the other hand, sees in the visual not a division, but an intertwining. The visual for Merleau-Ponty is an embodied place of sensuous encounter with the world. Lacan feels as if Merleau-Ponty wants to reach back to an original moment where we are closer to the world of flesh, where we are not plagued, seduced, and alienated by this virtual split. But Lacan says he doesn't believe there is any such ground.

Lacan is certainly critiquing Merleau-Ponty after depicting this moment at sea with the fisherman. But he says he finds his philosophical ambition quite touching, even moving: 'Merleau-Ponty wants to be wrapped in flesh like a mother's arms'. Suddenly, the mother appears! 'I know this desire. I hear it all the time', Lacan almost exclaims. Instead of her questioning or desirous gaze, what is there is a tender embrace, waiting for us.

Lacan's Real, however, is the opposite of a tender embrace. Merleau-Ponty's search for the visual turned him more and more towards painting. Yet, even the story of his beloved painter – Cezanne – is shrouded in alienation rather than sensuality. Cezanne, Merleau-Ponty remarks, suffered greatly during his life, having many depressive breakdowns. For Merleau-Ponty, his 'schizoid temperament' and 'frozenness' is why he was able to search for the true 'expression' of nature, to search the whole of our exterior. Perhaps today, we are closer to Cezanne, stuck searching the whole of our exterior without the privilege or talent for painting? The incessant gazing is looking to cure itself, encounter something Real, find a means to move into expression.

In the end, aesthetics can't solve Merleau-Ponty's philosophical problem exactly the way he wishes; it can't bring him back into his mother's embrace. But still, turning to art still does something for him, as it no doubt did for Cezanne. Lacan notes that it appears to calm him down, cauterising his wounded searching, his infinite demand, for his mother's flesh. Merleau-Ponty, he says, imagines Cezanne's brush-strokes – *those little blues, those little browns, those little whites* (Lacan Seminar XI, p. 110) – like a lullaby he repeats to himself, offering to him a substitute for the object he demands, just as a mother mediates the immediacy of contact through singing songs or telling stories.

While envy, jealousy, competitive ambition are incited by the gaze, there might be a renunciation of some kind within it. *Invidia*, greed, comes from *videre* in Latin, to see. 'It is to this register of the eye as made desperate by the gaze that we must go if we are to grasp the taming, civilizing and fascinating power of the function of a picture', Lacan writes. This is what painting asks of the gaze: to throw itself down. 'If a bird were to paint would it not be by letting fall its feathers, a snake by casting off its scales, a tree by letting fall its leaves?' To see at the place of this fall.

Painters' gestures, Lacan notes, are movements that terminate. At some point a painting is declared finished, a terminus that gives to the gaze of its viewer a stopping point, a sense of the descent of desire, which is difficult to know. The *invidia* of the gaze is not merely to be jealous of what the other has – which, as I said, you don't really know much about – but an encounter with the fantastical image of a completeness closed upon itself that reaches a pitch of fury and then finds a means of stopping, laying down its arms.

Painting, Lacan says, demonstrates that there is no promised totality in what you see. Painting offers to its viewer a hole, an opening of the visual out from the gaze.

'Freud always stressed with infinite respect that he did not intend to settle the question of what it was in artistic creation that gave it its true value' (Lacan Seminar XI, p. 110). Sublimation assumes a value for Freud simply because there is something profitable in art for society. But that something remains enigmatic; Freud, Lacan reminds us, refused to say more than this.

Lacan, however, would like to take Freud's message slightly further: 'Broadly speaking, one can say that the work calms people, comforts them, by showing them that at least some of them can live from the exploitation of their desire' (Lacan Seminar XI, p. 111). The artist's exploitation of their desire solicits the viewer's desire in an experience of its rebirth and closure. This crossing proves that some are not only exploited by others, by civilisation, or hemmed in by their consciousness. Exile and exclusion, beyond the reach of one's mother's embrace, becomes an exit.

Lacan's missive regarding the taming of the gaze – *dompte regarde* – and the invocation of the 'some' who can live surprised me; it felt close to something we desperately need at the current moment. How to exit this demanding gaze towards and from our phones? So many renditions of the gaze stress the aspects of power and envy with respect to the visual, such as the male gaze, which only leaves you feeling more uneasy, more open to exploitation. Versions of Lacanian film analysis play with the split as dramatised on the screen, or between the screen and its viewer, inciting the gaze and hiding the subject of desire. But why not show us how desire meets with itself in these visual mediums, finds points of freedom and even a future, rather than simply being further duped?

What if the visual were an encounter with this temporality of looking with a stopping point, or this breaking apart of a totality? Certainly this is the direction that psychoanalysis goes. Merleau-Ponty too,

If there is a relation of the visible with itself that traverses me and constitutes me as a seer, this circle which I do not form, which forms me, this coiling over of the visible upon the visible, can traverse, animate other bodies as well as my own. And if I was able to understand how this wave arises within me, how the visible which is yonder is simultaneously my landscape, I can understand *a fortiori* that elsewhere it also closes over upon itself and that there are other landscapes besides my own.

(Merleau-Ponty, 1968, pp. 140–141)

Where Merleau-Ponty and Lacan meet on the visible beyond the gaze is the experience of its movement in time and space: a wave, an exigency that closes over upon itself, the descent of desire, and eventually, from this experience, a style of working.

Every generation has to ask how it fits, or not, into the picture of things. What or how were you excluded? The fact that we are never in the same place is a saving grace – *you never look at me from the place that I see you.* If there is the cry of recrimination from one generation to another, it is a testimony to this space, the chiasm. I am reminded of a moment with one of my patients who protested that he couldn't see where we were going with all of this. How was he going to get out of this psychoanalysis that had taken over him? I suddenly recalled a dream from earlier in the week where I left him a handwritten note and repeated what I had written to him: I'll see you there.

This version of seeing across spatial and temporal distance, the encounter with something unknown, and yet a meeting point, feels different from symptomatic incessant gazing, doubting, frozen searching for an object, demand for the totality of the Other. It is seeing as moving. Seeing as *rendezvous*. Seeing in the future tense. It may be a fantasy, but I like to imagine that this younger generation who grew up on the internet are looking for something different: not critique, but what can be ameliorated; not outrage, but what might calm us down; not the amplification of alienation, but the search for what gives us a feeling of a possible life.

We are willingly giving ourselves over to exploitation. The internet now sees all that we do; we give ourselves over to it for exploitation in the name of convenience and to continue looking at it all. This makes these questions about the visible invaluable, as Merleau-Ponty writes, amidst 'the debris of an unknown celebration'. He reminds us: '*We never get away from our life. We never see our ideas or our freedom face to face*' (Merleau-Ponty, 1993, p. 25, italics added). We have to keep working.

Fantastical gazes that attack the maternal

The particular American brand of freedom – a fantastical image once referred to by psychoanalyst Erik Erikson as a frontier mentality, where to stop moving is the equivalent of dying – has long had truculent wheels. Since the pandemic, I feel as if 'freedom' is on overdrive. Erikson noted that the American hatred for the elderly seemed to spring from this image of freedom as free mobility since they can't move quickly anymore, a problem only momentarily solved by RV or mobile home culture. The pandemic, with its lockdown and mask mandates, and the requirement that we do this *for* the elderly, seems ripe for a renewal of this fantastical image – right up to the Capitol Hill riots. The spectre of death during the pandemic was strong, especially in those early days of such intense uncertainty, but our survival seems not to have left us thinking about the preciousness of life, nor with a more positive regard for life in common, but rather the reverse. Why?

For one, our choices were revealed not within the framework of a positive image of my freedom to do X, Y, or Z, but rather in the framework of a negative image of being free *from*: harm, humiliating exposure, or excessive threat of death, which means a limitation on personal freedom. Secondly, the pandemic meant much of life moved even more online, which also feels backlit by a fantasy of free movement. The anonymous looking and posting online, as we know, has led to less regard for community and greater hostilities, racism, and misanthropy. One needs to ask if envy and jealousy are the main culprits: for accepting personal limitations when those limitations are far from equal across class, has been obviated by the pandemic. And what else do we do online but look and look at other people's lives, ideas, self-representations?

In the end, the idea of choice would better be thought without the burden of a fantasy of freedom. Choice is more about the world bringing itself to bear, the messy entanglements of life, the inequities of history and our ethical decisions, than about some ideal of being unencumbered. I've helped patients make hard decisions in their lives. Patients, after the labour of speaking, often say to me, 'Only you know'. What they mean is only I know how difficult it is to arrive where they have, because I've listened to them do so. This gift by psychoanalysis needs protection, meaning the protection of desire as a set of choices authorised by one-self alone. Desire, so understood, needs protecting because it is fragile – at its core, unjustifiable – and the way for us to take responsibility for the choices we do make and to accept the losses they incur. We can then, presumably, have greater empathy for the difficult choices of others.

Otherwise, we simply live in the volatile realm of fantasy, trapped by the vicis-situdes of the gaze, which undergirds violent feelings about the desires of oth-ers – what they are doing that makes us feel so threatened. Melanie Klein, one of the first psychoanalysts to work with children, spoke about the primal scene – the fantasy-filled image of a first, shocking exposure to adult sexuality, often as sex between parents or a stand-in for them – as a nightmare of endless procreation, the woman's womb a nest of babies. The primal scene fantasy is often the presumed conception of a dreaded sibling. Freud was attentive to how children feel power-fully displaced by their parents' love for one another and by the birth of other babies. 'Many children who believed themselves securely enthroned in the unshak-able affection of their parents', he writes, 'have been cast down by a single blow from all the heavens of their imaginary omnipotence' (Freud, 1919, p. 186).

The psychoanalyst Wilfred Bion made the joke that whenever two people are seen, one immediately imagines they are having sex and wants to stop them. The joke is that we cannot stand the knowledge that our parents' desires are, at a certain point, off limits to us. They belong to them, to their life and circumstances, their intimacies, errors, confusions. When we want to curb someone else's desire, psy-choanalysis hears the child's confrontation with adult sexual realities, which can become a palpable hatred of sexuality altogether.

In psychoanalysis, numerous 'universal' fantasies begin with the primal scene. "A Child Is Being Beaten" is the strange title of Freud's paper on some of the sex-ual fantasies his patients revealed only after many years of psychoanalysis and with great difficulty. Several of his patients, he writes, used this shameful, subject-less sentence to describe a fantasy of sadomasochistic enjoyment. 'One wished to carry the investigation further', he writes:

Who was the child that was being beaten? The one who was himself producing the phantasy or another? Was it always the same child or as often as not a dif-ferent one? Who was it that was beating the child? A grown up person? And if so, who? Or did the child imagine that he himself was beating another one? No information was produced for clearing up all these questions, nothing but the one timid reply: 'I know nothing more about it: a child is being beaten'.

(Freud, 1919, p. 181).

So what is this beating fantasy? Why is it so difficult to articulate?

After working with his patients, Freud concluded that the fantasy has three phases. In the first phase, the father is seen beating another child, a scene that feels like an early memory. Freud describes this vision as 'not clearly sexual, not in itself sadistic, but yet the stuff from which both will later come' (Freud, 1919, p. 187). The nascent sexuality and sadism is found not in the act of beating itself, but in the enjoyment at seeing another child being punished. Seeing them beaten allows the subject to imagine that the parent loves not that other child but oneself alone.

In phase two – the most difficult to access – the image is now of the father beating the subject as a child. The second phase of the fantasy is an attempt at being part of the action of the scene, indeed being the object of the action. This means admitting sexual enjoyment along with the punishment and guilt one feels for having it. Freud says that this phase succumbs to repression almost entirely.

Phase three is the final and most conscious form of the fantasy, 'a child is being beaten'. It creates a pure dissociation, the subject leaving the scene, leaving their childhood, leaving their body and state of arousal, and becoming a pure voyeur. All parties appear as anonymous, generalised others. Lacan even comments that one is reduced to the object at the most extreme limit, namely the eye and its screen. Seemingly, one enjoys by screening out all feelings of terror, jealousy, and rage.

Condensed into the image of an adult beating a child, then, are so many surprising elements that the paper feels utterly wild. Importantly, Freud notes, these fantasies aren't the musings of perverse patients but common daydreams, perhaps even universal scripts, that graft childhood experience onto cultural mores. There are also the outlines of a traumatic memory, according to Freud, of seeing other children punished, and wondering: What is loved and hated by these adults? What is good, and what is bad? What, in essence, makes for authority?

The fantasy offers a potential identification with power, to be the one who beats as opposed to the one who is beaten. This does the work of hiding a feeling of utter helplessness and subjection, indeed objectification within processes of life. The difficult feelings concerning what we want from another person, making us open to their blows, are there but screened out. By taking the subject out of the scene altogether, the third phase provides still greater distance. Being everywhere and nowhere in the plotlines, we shirk responsibility for our desire.

Sex sounds to children like rhythmic beating, heavy breathing, scary moaning. Pregnancy and birth are likewise terrifyingly incomprehensible. Beating is not only the action of masturbation – beating off, excitement's periodicity – but also a stand-in for the experience of insufficiency in the face of sexual reality. In typical Freudian fashion, we are getting closer to incestuous wishes: the child's desire for love and jealousy towards potential rivals for this love. We enjoy seeing them beat, or, beat ourselves out of the picture into the position of an onlooker to manage this difficult feeling of jealousy.

Why does the father have such a prominent role? One may assume that it is because Freud's patients were women and the fantasy is oedipal – directed at the parent of the opposite sex. But in fact, the patients were both men and women, and Freud speculates that the father is a substitute or screen for the fantasy's real object, which is the mother: the first powerful object of dependency and attachment for a child of either sex. Because the mother is the one whose attention we most covet and most fear, the fantasy of being 'the desired one' has echoes of a fantasised return to the helpless position of an infant and ultimately a return to the womb. This, for Freud, is the most narcissistic fantasy: seeking to reoccupy the body of the mother. But, paradoxically, it is also a scene that explodes you, going where you were not and could not be, to a time before you were born.

Allow me to jump to contemporary events. This sibling rivalry and wish to reoccupy the body of the mother, displaced into a beating fantasy, has become a shocking and regressive reality in the United States with the overturning of *Roe* v. *Wade*. Following the pandemic, the concerns and inequity of care in my country, it feels like a real blow against women, especially minority women, at a time when resources for the care of children have been stripped to a minimum. We may force children to be born, but we do not take care of them, or their mothers, afterwards.

What is this hatred? While we must respect the human capacity for fantasising, the worry is its unanalysed enactment against others in a political realm. As Pier Paolo Pasolini wrote, in an essay against abortion:

> I am . . . profoundly disturbed by the legalization of abortion, because I, like many others, consider it to be a legalization of homicide. In my dreams, and in my everyday life – and this is something that I have in common with all men – I live my prenatal life, my happy immersion in the maternal waters: I know that I already existed there.
>
> (Pasolini, 1975)

The images of a filmmaker, and a brilliant one. But if he lives in the womb day and night, *it is* as pure fantasy. Another image of being wrapped in a mother's flesh?

'A Child Is Being Aborted': this is the fantasy at the centre of the overturning of *Roe* v. *Wade*. There is the all-too-obvious identification with the foetus that, like the child in the fantasy described by Freud's patients, finds itself unwanted, no longer the desired one, cast out of its 'happy immersion in the maternal waters'. Retaliating against this affront, the speaker seeks to move the hand of law to rule out all abortion, as if all women wanted to rid themselves of babies. A circle's two ends meet – me now and me then – in a womb, declaring, 'I will not be aborted!'

The image of saving the life of the unborn provides cover both for negating maternal power and for denying one's own aggression against one's rivals for the parents' love. This self-redemption is ultimately accomplished through an appeal to law and order. 'I should not be surprised', Freud writes, 'if it were one day possible to prove that the same phantasy is the basis of the delusional litigiousness of paranoia' (Freud, 1919, p. 195).

For a doctor to intervene in the body of a pregnant woman according to her wishes – yet another primal scene – he will now have to consult a lawyer, who will have to consult the courts, all the way up. Now that this interventionist policy is sanctioned, there will be no end to the intrusive voyeurism taking hold in the form of abortion bounty laws; no prohibition of the will to make women suffer their sexuality on behalf of foetal personhood. The first self-declared 'sanctuary city for the unborn' was Waskom, Texas, in 2019, and more than 40 other cities have followed suit. The fantasy of life made and destroyed at will authorises the targeted destruction of an individual's desire – its enigma, its historical exigencies, its place as a choice among a series of unknown and overdetermined constraints.

Against legislation that generalises all women into mothers and all of sexuality into reproductive aims, the practice of psychoanalysis is determined by the singular history of each patient. We protect the choices that emerge from that history, not as individual rights but as decisions understandable only through careful articulation. Psychoanalysis is a kind of sanctuary city for desire, but it is a place where you cannot live; rather, you must find the way it lives in you. Fantasies will be read, examined, taken apart, unearthing the anxiety that provides them with ammunition.

Having a child gives rise to a raw, naked fear, staring down the utter contingency of bringing life into the world: the contingency of conceiving, of who the child will grow up to be, of the world it is born into. While we might imagine other pasts or futures for ourselves, so many lives unlived, as the psychoanalyst Adam Philips called them, we cannot know what is in the hearts of others unless we listen to them, very carefully. Otherwise, it is fantasy.

Phillips says he worries not so much about unlived lives – we all have them by the bucketful – but about their capacity to take over actual life and degrade it. The overturning of *Roe* v. *Wade* and the abortion bans to come mean we've gone a step further: we are codifying into law the fantasy of unlived life and imposing it, as if this is the way to win back our mothers, this sadistic vigilance over their desire. Perhaps there is an attempt here – as with all sexual fantasies – to get closer to what it feels like to be on the other side of a divide: there with her. The problem is that this is being done through what I can only call a beating fantasy.

Inside the gaze is history

How did we get here? How have we constructed life as envious gazing and the reassertion of control over women's bodies? Where did sensuality go in the outlines of such perverse enjoyment in beating, gazing, hating, coveting? I stumbled upon a psychoanalytic reconstruction of America that was fascinating and felt oddly explanatory. It begins with a particularly American fantasy about mothers, or 'mom', as a revered but rejected figure in Erik Erikson's much-lauded *Childhood and Society*, written in 1950.

Erikson starts with the observation that one society seemingly cannot understand another's sublimations, especially those that concerned passed-down methods of child rearing. One culture accuses the other of 'doing deliberate harm to their children'. Importantly, these child-rearing practices are communal and sedimented over time; practices that are disappearing in our internet-driven, globalised age of information.

In the 1950s, especially with a confrontation with extensive immigration in America, the image of the other's ways of parenting immediately evoked condemnation. Erikson notes that one culture looks at what the other does regarding punishment (or a lack of it, which seems to require greater propriety), then judges these others while validating one's own measures within the same sphere. A kind of *my beating fantasy is more correct than your beating fantasy.* We cannot see the picture that we are in. And moreover, what we look at isn't what we want to see.

The judgment is instantaneous. A pure gaze and image. What can never be seen, can only be understood with care and effort and listening and dialogue, are the sedimentations within a culture whose practices create positive and unique conditions around the taming of a child's sexual impulses. Every child-rearing practice creates positive outcomes of one kind or another that attempt to fit a child within a certain framework. Erikson surmises that some sense for the different sensualities and forms of permitted enjoyment of other cultures is behind the condemnation.

This leads to a situation of complete bi-directional misunderstanding and misrecognition, one subculture condemning the other. In Erikson's work with indigenous populations assimilating into white schools, the mutual misunderstanding fuelled increasing distrust and contempt. While the indigenous populations certainly had cause to distrust whites, in the case of their children attending white schools, it wasn't this history of violence and oppression in the foreground but confusion around the specific ways whites managed their own children, who seemed to them over-indulged. An actual sense for history of why whites parent the way they do would have been useful to the indigenous, who gave their own children conflicting commands when it came to a place they might occupy in white schools.

Erikson found the same conundrum within psychoanalysis and psychiatry, whose occupational prejudice was blaming mothers for making people mentally ill. Especially with psychotic children, the idea was always that it was the mother's fault and the analyst would have done a better job. This, according to Erikson, leads to a complete degradation of the value of a culture, or the efforts of any given family. The causal explanations, the easy assessment of what are the supposed costs for an individual, are blaming and self-congratulatory. The assessment relies on an outside gaze, and the psychiatrists can't see the picture that includes them.

For example, Erikson wonders how this blame of moms begins for psychiatrists. What does rejecting tons of men as 'psychoneurotics' unable to go to Europe and fight have to do with it? The Americans who, underneath their stereotyped smiles and countenance of self-control, were found to lack the spontaneity that would keep them both intact and flexible under extreme circumstances; well, their answer was that Mom did it. 'Case history after case history states that the patient had a cold mother, a dominant mother, a rejecting mother – or a hyper-possessive, over-protective one' (Erikson, 1950, p. 261). The implication is that the child wasn't attended to in the way that was needed, and they imply that the father was dominated as well, and that whatever good he did offer to the children was spoilt because of what he 'took' from the mom. One should surmise a question here of assessing what a mother gives and to whom.

Erikson writes:

Gradually what had begun as a spontaneous movement in thousands of clinical files has become manifest literary spirt in books decrying the mothers of this country as 'Moms' and as a 'generation of vipers'. Who is this Mom? And how could she become an excuse for all that is rotten in the state of the nation and a subject of literary temper tantrums?

(Erikson, 1950)

The tone reached a pitch of vengeful triumph and moralistic punitiveness. Moms, says this beating fantasy, are sexually frigid, rejecting of their children, and unduly dominant. All causality has become linked with blame.

Erikson is quite wry. He knows this has something to do with the hold that the ideal of mental health has gained in this country. He points out that when the child of some psychiatrist friends was asked what he wanted to be when he grew up, the child said, 'a patient'. Erikson adds, perhaps because he said it, he doesn't have to play out this tragic fantasy. In general, Erikson says, the 'psychoneurotic' American solider that felt unprepared for life often implicitly blamed his mother. And perhaps all the experts began to agree with him. But it is also true that the road from the American Main Street to the European foxhole was long, and he finds it odd that we blame American families for the failures of this long road, while denying credit to those mothers for the sons who did overcome that distance. Either way, we have a scene of intense sibling rivalry.

We must, he says, take apart the visual gestalt that forms this revered and rejected image of Mom, the moment of a kind of visual closure that lends support to contempt. We must break down the image into a composite series of traits. 'No woman', he writes, 'consciously aspires to be such a Mom, and yet, she may find that her experience converges on this Gestalt, as if she were forced to assume the role'. This is what we can learn from psychiatry:

1. Mom is the unquestioned authority on mores in home and community, but remains in her own way vain, egotistical in her demands, and infantile in her emotions.
2. She blames her children, never herself.
3. She maintains the discrepancy between a child and adult, but without appealing to any higher meaning. She herself is a bad example.
4. She shows hostility to any free expression of the most naïve forms of sensual or sexual pleasure, and makes it clear that anyone sexually demanding is a bore. Yet as she grows older, she refuses to sacrifice her claims to sexual power and is addicted to sexual displays in books, magazines, movies, and gossip.
5. She teaches self-restraint but is unable to restrain herself, particularly orally.
6. She expects her children to be hard on themselves, but is a hypochondriac when it comes to her own well-being.
7. She proclaims the superior value of tradition but herself hates getting old, and in fact is mortally afraid of a status which was the fruit of a rich life and a status to be admired – a grandmother.

Erikson says that this is the perfect image of a series of contradictions, not of moms or women, but of America. Within the image of reviled mothers, constructed by the contempt of jealous children, is a picture of a particular social world riven with historical contradictions.

'Mom', he writes, 'of course is only a stereotyped character of existing contradictions which have emerged from intense, rapid, and as yet unintegrated changes in American history' (Erikson, 1950, p. 268). We can now reconstruct the history that was captured in this image of Mom who is being beaten by Americans. Erikson wants to begin with the frontier,

> We would have to retrace history back to the time when it was up to the American woman to evolve one common tradition, and to base on it the education of children and style of home life; when it was up to her to establish new habits of sedentary life on a continent populated by men who in their countries of origin had not wanted to be 'fenced in'. In fear of ever again acquiescing to an outer or inner autocracy, these men insisted on keeping their new cultural identity tentative to a point where women had to become autocratic in their demands for some order.
>
> (Erikson, 1950, p. 263)

The community, he conjectures, would have fallen apart without these finer graces introduced by women. She must have adjusted unconsciously to this continent and avoided maternal protectionism, which would weaken frontiersmen.

Added to this picture of the burdens placed on Mom's shoulders was puritanism. And then, during a short course of history, we had forced migration of native population, unchecked immigration, industrialisation, urbanisation, class stratification, and finally, female emancipation. This put puritanism on the defensive. Beyond defining sexual sin for full-blooded and strong-willed people it extended itself to the entire sphere of sensuality, spreading its frigidity and hatred over the tasks of pregnancy, childbirth, nursing, and child rearing. All the way up to the overturning of *Roe* v. *Wade*.

Sensuality and desire are guarded against with a vigilant eye. Men, says Erikson, would not have learned the goodness of sensuality before learning to hate its sinful uses. Along with hating sin, they must have mistrusted life. This makes for a puritanism without faith or zest. Meanwhile, the contradictions between staying or continuing to move, towns and urbanisation, well, Erikson says, you had to either follow – or stay behind and brag louder. This defence against sedentary life is what Erikson thinks gave ageing and old age such a bad name in this country. Sensuality and weakness, signs of continuing life and the precariousness of desire, are detestable.

Children of older generations, the first Americans of immigrant families, emulated in the Americans around them what they did not experience themselves as children. This often made them their 'parents' cultural parents', equivalent to the self-made man. This was only reinforced by industrialisation and class stratification. This brought a rigidity into a new training method for children that began to emulate machines in the model of absolute standardisation. Middle-class mothers found themselves 'standardizing and over-adjusting children who were later expected to personify virile individuality which had been one of the outstanding characteristics of the Americans. Instead, we were in danger of creating a mass-produced mask of individuality' (Erikson, 1950, p. 269).

If that was not enough, the European aristocratic ideal of the lady as someone who doesn't need to work, translated in America as a woman who is too childlike and uninformed to do so. This is now met with a demand for emancipation. While this should have signalled greater equality, it became a pretence of sameness in equipment, meaning the right to mannish behaviour for all. In the end, then, Erikson says, 'Momism' is really misplaced paternalism. Mothers in America found themselves having to step into the role of grandfathers, as fathers abdicated their role in the family, cultural life, and education, cultivating their role as freeborn sons. This is, according to Erikson, American's fragmentary Oedipus complex, one that cannot even acknowledge an archaic sensual attachment to the mother, certainly cannot understand women's desire bound by necessity; a cause for increasing generational rivalry and jealousy in the old oedipal sense, but here twisted into this attack on outsiders (immigrants who do not fit the American mould), the old, and women, in the name of free-born sons.

What is incredible in this drawn-out description of what hides behind the image of mothers reviled by Erikson is to see the oedipal scene as intact by means of being pulverised and twisted. An image that expresses oedipal vicissitudes while screening out all historical particularity, especially historical contradictions. Perhaps what any good phantasm achieves. By the end: 'Mom', they say, has let everyone down. This appears quickly in psychoanalysis according to Erikson under the proud exterior performance of autonomy by Americans. Dad is allowed to be distantly admired, but not really known. Erikson calls this the silent schizoid character of Americans who go from an exuberant sense of initiative to a silent withdrawal. The old oedipal complaints of inhibition are complaints in this country of not having an identity – and indeed, they do not. America is action and motion up to a breaking point, after which psychosomatic disturbance or delinquency beckons.

Importantly, Erikson says he has had the chance as an analyst to look deeply, and with time, you finally find the 'mortal self-accusation that it was the child who abandoned the mother, because he had been in such a hurry to become independent' (Erikson, 1950, p. 268). And this mortal self-accusation would in part be true, part of a culture of the pure repudiation of women. This mortal accusation opens the door to increasing sociopathy according to Erikson, which follows a hollowing out of ideals that will not summon forth the intelligence of its own youth, nor provide them with any authentic feeling for a valued historical transmission between generations. This is the crack that opens a vacuum – indeed, one that has been filled to the brink with gazing at others' lives with jealousy and contempt, displaced the most cruelly onto women who are blamed for not making good on these feelings.

The mortal self-accusation is transferred to rival others and mothers and must be sustained with vigilance. As psychoanalytic theorist Lee Edelman says of his puritanical vision of children whose innocence it is the job of mothers to keep (just as they must keep all babies) – what we have here is an image of the fascist face of the baby. This puritanical image undergirds much of the violence of the American ideal of freedom and autonomy. Here I think we finally see how this demand for the mother, an infinitely jealous gaze, and the attack on women's desire, has brought us to our historical moment in thrall to the image. Is it any wonder, then, that suicide rates amongst women and children have increased over 40 per cent from 2010 to 2025, especially since the onset of social media?

Reference list

Erikson, E.H. (1950). *Childhood and society.* W.W. Norton & Co.

Freud, S. (1919). 'A child is being beaten': A contribution to the study of the origin of sexual perversions. In *The standard edition of the complete psychological works of Sigmund Freud. Vol. XVII (1917–1919): An infantile neurosis and other works* (pp. 175–204). Hogarth Press.

Lacan, J. (1966). *Unpublished translation of seminar XIV the logic of fantasy 1966–1967.* Cormac Gallagher at LacaninIreland.com.

Lacan J. (1998). *The seminar of Jacques Lacan: Book XI four fundamental concepts of psychoanalysis.* Alan Sheridan (Trans.) and Jacques-Alain Miller (Ed.).W.W. Norton & Co.

Merleau-Ponty, M. (1968). *The visible and the invisible* (A. Lingis, Trans.). Northwestern University Press.

Merleau-Ponty, M. (1993). Phenomenology and painting: 'Cezanne's doubt'. In G.A. Johnson (Ed.), *The Merleau-Ponty aesthetics reader: Philosophy and painting.* Northwestern University Press.

Pasolini, P. (1975, January 19). I am against abortion. *Corriere della Sera.*

Chapter 9

Jealousy

The good, the bad, and the social

Carmen Wright

Melanie Klein makes a distinction between envy and jealousy in *Envy and Gratitude* (1975, p. 81). Envy aims at destroying the good, whereas jealousy, albeit in a destructive way, aims at preserving it. Jealousy is not simply about dispossessing others but about maintaining what one 'has', or grieving what has been 'taken', both of which include investment in something *desired*, or in Klein's vocabulary, in 'the good'. Envy, then, does not reckon with loss (whether actual, perceived, or potential) in the way jealousy does – envy destroys so as *not* to lose, is aimed not at gain but at the diminishment of one's losses, or, to put it more sympathetically, levelling the playing field.[1]

Even if we disagree about jealousy forging around a kind of goodness, or think Klein's bifurcation of envy and jealousy a little neat, there is something intuitive to her invocation of ethics. It does not take long for most discussions about jealousy to venture into questions of whether it is a force for good or bad,[2] some noting its absence betrays an eerie indifference, others emphasising its prominence in instances of domestic abuse and even murder. If we are jealous, or our partner or friend is jealous, does this reveal an impassioned attachment, or a disregard for the sanctity of our differences? Is jealousy on the side of desire, which is to say, facing up to the realness of others' desires; or is it on the side of delimiting desires, on curbing, trying to contain or even control them? Do we owe loved ones any knowledge of our desires, and if we don't, wouldn't this harm the social realm? One moment jealousy is juvenile, the next its tolerance seems wise, seems to usher us uncomfortably into the proper stakes of relating.

Psychoanalysts also tend to fall into two camps on this question. Whereas for Klein as well as Winnicott, as we'll see, to feel jealous is an important milestone necessary to our capacity for love, for Ernest Jones it obstructs it, since we perceive loved ones as instruments to plug a narcissistic deficiency (the jealous aim at *being* loved, not loving).[3] Perhaps jealousy's apparent bipolarity is due to its being a powerful support for the social and asocial alike (depending on how it is functioning for the person). Or maybe it is due to the fact that the feeling is itself always both: to be jealous is to be acutely conflicted, Winnicott (2017 [1950]) noticed. He meant that we love and we hate at once, and thus we are mired in complex ethical dilemmas. But we might also point to the special kind of headache that

DOI: 10.4324/9781032637549-9

feeling jealous involves: we know what we demand is impossible, unsustainable, that we could not abide it – and yet we equally feel ourselves to be righteous, to be dangling on the precipice of abandonment to admit the other's split attention. Is jealousy the affective component of this impasse, an outcome of the conflict between individual freedom and our duty to others? The other side of the coin to guilt perhaps, where we imagine ourselves to be agents taunted by that duty. With jealousy, we imagine ourselves to be the objects agents leave behind, yet in both cases it is our freedom – our separateness, and the distance and inscrutability this opens up – which is the problem.

We live in especially confusing times today when it comes to ethics. The galvanising of MeToo, Black Lives Matter and LGBTQ+ activism since the mid-2010s made pre-existing conversations about the way race, gender, and sexuality affect lives gradually more mainstream. Equally, terms that help depict, sometimes to label, psychical life – such as 'trauma', 'mental health', 'neurodiversity', and so on – are far more commonplace. Which is to say lived vulnerabilities that had previously been siphoned off from public life, seen as an *individual's* problem, are now talking points with acknowledged material consequences, regardless of the plentiful debates these complex subjects evoke. Resultantly, the culture is arguably better attuned to our ethical obligations to others, newly sensitive to everyone's right to be freed *from* the barriers that people face, some more than others.

At the same time, we're also still rather attached to the perhaps longer-serving, neoliberal freedom *to* – the ring that is drawn around subjective experience with which to do, say, and want as we please. These two freedoms converge and conflict not only to produce culture wars, but also to produce apparent impasses in personal relationships, where the difficulty in dividing up who owes what to whom is no longer looked at as a relational hazard, but as something we are desperate to unscramble, be rid of. Perhaps this explains the mass appeal of therapy-speak, which appears to have it all figured out: just communicate your boundaries! Although these days the use of 'boundaries' is caveated with 'I hate the term, but', since it has been shown, in fact, to know no bounds. The most bizarre example of this must be the Jonah Hill fiasco, in which he requested his girlfriend refrain from posting revealing pictures of herself on the internet, something which he argued trespassed *his* boundaries.

The scramble to resolve the problem of these competing freedoms also sees our freedom *to* sometimes pose as our freedom *from*. For Jonah Hill, for instance, asking for what he wanted was inverted into a demand to be freed from what he didn't want. This inversion allows for a landscape in which competing points of view are replaced by claiming there is only one legitimate perspective, alongside an unsurprisingly greater sense of its fragility, of its being at risk of damage and violation. Maybe this is simply a misuse of asserting boundaries; but it seems also to highlight their arbitrary usage, and the way the freedom problem has and will always be a minefield attached to relating. Even if the 'boundary' solution – that it is reasonable to curb one person's freedom *to* at the point when it infringes on somebody else's freedom *from* – didn't chronically slip out of bounds, it is powerless in the face of jealous possessiveness. Perhaps it even acquiesces to it, since it encourages a turning away from others' desires, at the very same time as claiming to know them. And surely focusing on protecting one another's freedoms as though they are isolated, spatial entities owned by each subject only obfuscates the way desires tend to affect and generate each other, the way we are each dependent on each other's desires for our own to function?

Indeed, the metaphors invoked to smooth over the freedom problem, supposed to liberate us from jealousies, projections, or the emotional dumping of others – of boundaries which ought not be trespassed, of being 'at capacity' – are generally linked to the vocabulary of property; of occupancy, ownership, a space that can be clearly identified, carved up, possessed. The very same conceit that produces envy and insidious forms of jealousy (as soon as something is imagined as being *had*, a fantasy of *total* possession can follow). And yet, *there is also something about jealousy that throws that conceit into relief.* 'Jealousy is about wanting to know more about the people we love, and knowing we'll never be able to', as the psychoanalyst to the protagonist of Lauren Elkin's novel, *Scaffolding*, puts it (2024, p. 31). What hidden depths, what secret garden, has the other been enjoying when the subject is not or was not there? What, in other words, archaeological treasures reside beneath the neat boundaries of our property?

Jealousy's bidirectionality is implicit in Freud's 'Some Neurotic Mechanisms in Paranoia, Jealousy and Homosexuality' (1922), when he makes a point of distinguishing a perfectly ordinary, not to say appropriate, kind of jealousy from two others which perform suppressive acrobatics (see introduction). Freud, Lacan, and Winnicott all notice that this former jealousy helps the subject contend with a kind of realness, with the Other, yet which of course also involves grief, dismay, disappointment (in a useful way). We could say the *bad* kind of jealousy, the kind which Freud wanted to call 'projective' jealousy – to say nothing of delusional – is its opposite. It doubles down to deny what the 'good' jealousy mournfully revealed, refusing to partake in the silent pact this knowledge gives rise to (that you shouldn't ask questions you don't want the answers to). It wants to know nothing of the minefield of relating, of the problems of wrestling freedom from our duties to others, and instead it is as though the knowledge of our own and others' freedom *to* is experienced as an infringement on the subject's right to freedom *from* incurring suffering (the suffering of being separate, which normal jealousy showed up in the first place!). It is in a way the fact that projective jealousy unconsciously registers but disavows normal jealousy, which makes it particularly hard to handle. The subject seems to recognise that any unlikely claim that they could possess somebody else's desires is just that – unlikely – hence how their beloved's reassurances usually rattle, rather than settle, their jealous feelings.

The matter of jealousy's *good* function of course returns to what is for me the most important contribution psychoanalysis has made – something we need psychoanalysis to grasp – how subjects emerge in the first place, and how we come to register our difference from, yet the realness of, other subjects. Some link this to the oedipal complex, some want to highlight pre-oedipal milestones, but the important idea for our purposes is that this is a process that passes through a phase of imagined possession, according to most psychoanalytic theorists regardless of orientation.

For D.W. Winnicott, famously, there is no such thing as a baby. This is because at the start of life, there is no separation: no 'me' and no 'you'. In episodes from a radio series broadcast in 1960 entitled *The Ordinary Devoted Mother and Her Children*, he hears from a group of mothers about their experience of jealousy amongst their children, linking these observations to an account of how separation emerges. He suggests the analogy of a slogan for theatre tickets – 'You want the best seats; we have them' – for how jealousy emerges for the infant, in the form of a similar two-part sequence: 'I have the best mother; and you want her' (2017, p. 53). In the beginning,

> the mother, and everything that stands for her, is taken for granted by the infant. Then comes 'I have the best mother', and this marks the dawn of the baby's understanding that the mother is not just part of the baby's self, but that she comes to the baby from outside, and she might not come, and there could be other mothers. For the baby the mother now *becomes a possession*, and one that can be held on to or dropped.
>
> (p. 53)

This is not immediate but requires time to develop – only later does the second part come in, the '*and you want her*'.[4] But, he says, even then, 'this is not jealousy yet, it is a matter of defended possession. Here the child holds on tight. . . . Then at last comes the recognition that the central possession, mother, can belong to someone else' (p. 53).

At the risk of rushing through decades of intricate theorisation, we see here how for Winnicott, in some sense the *realness* of the mother,[5] her existence in the world outside the infant, begins with a rudimentary experience of jealousy (as defended possession), which itself relies on a dawning recognition that what we have can be lost or taken. By the same token, it is as though jealousy proper is destined to be heir to the ability to encounter this realness: that her desire is its *own thing*, which the infant can have only limited influence over, meaning now it is not the possession of her under threat, but the bearing of her love.

So, the movement of the mother exceeding her status as a possession and into a being with agency[6] happens *only after* it is recognised that she can belong, however momentarily, to somebody or something else. Her 'belonging' to another may expose that she never belonged to the infant, that she may not be a *belonging* at all, that it is all far more complex and confusing. It is this painful realisation that gives jealousy its severity, where the infant is seriously grief-stricken – considered in all its starkness, Juliet Mitchell argues, the 'terrible twos' better describes the *infant's* experience: something terrible happens *to* the toddler, a trauma, 'and it cannot cope' (p. 14). It is this which the toddler responds to with tantrums and any manner of refusals (to eat, sleep, walk, talk . . .). For Winnicott, this is the moment when 'the child is now one of the people who wants and is no longer one of those who have. It is somebody else who has' (pp. 53–54).

Like Mitchell's recent theory of the sibling trauma (2023), Lacan thought siblings, or little others (alter egos) – rivals for the mother's affection – kickstart this process. Lacan, as Winnicott did, notes the central role this painful experience of dethronement has in the infant's ability to identify with others, to put themselves in their shoes – which is to say, to reckon with the realness of others' desires. It is fundamental for sociability to be established; and jealousy's absence, by the same token, risks the subject's never quite entering the social and remaining cut off, caught up in a land of illusions (if not total delusion).

Winnicott is particularly sensitive to the inordinate task the mother has of dealing in her realness only gradually (too early and the infant is 'not in a position to have regard for the other; to ask them to recognise the mother's need would be to inflict damage on them', Emily Ogden paraphrases in *On Not Knowing*); keeping it back until, perhaps, the infant themselves encounters jealousy, at which point *they go looking for her realness*. On a recent trip, my friend reported that her almost three-year-old had begun to ask her, every day, 'Are you ok?'. When his sister (approaching one year old and not yet weaned) received their mother's attention, it was unbearable for him to witness. Is this concurrence of what appears to be an intense jealousy alongside a tender consideration of his mother's inner reality, of her feelings and her wants, mere coincidence?

It is hard not to notice that Winnicott's framing of this period, when the infant both registers something about what is real and by the same token loses a phantasmatic land of plenty, resonates strongly with the story of Eden – what else are Adam and Eve, banished from Eden, but people *who now want, and no longer have*? This is a motif we see everywhere in culture too – the red pill/blue pill divergence in *The Matrix* also comes to mind: would you rather hold on to an illusion that keeps you comfortable, or gain consciousness about the world that necessarily undermines your comfort, your centrality, causing the knowledge you thought you held to dissolve into a gaping ignorance?

And, of course, it is the symbol of weaning which stands in for that transition. Apt, then, that, as Emily Ogden notices in her essay 'How to Milk', in *The Matrix* 'all the people, from babies to adults [are] umbilically connected to the great machine that feeds them, [who] look like nothing so much as fetuses that failed either to be born or die' (2022, p. 27). Unsurprising too, perhaps, that a problem with weaning – its arrival too early or painfully – has been linked to jealousy, most notably by Joan Riviere (1932). Riviere theorised that an oral envy, a feeling of having been deprived of the breast which is now given to the other, can give rise to sadistic urges which the later jealous subject attributes to the other, by whom they begin to feel threatened. If we cast aside the restrictive debates about the timing of the oedipal complex, or that of whether it's really all about the resource of mother's milk, which Lacan of course dismissed, it's possible to see a through line that connects what Riviere noticed to the *disillusionment* that seems to play a role in this 'good' jealousy. In a way it ceases to matter if deprivation did or was imagined to have occurred; what matters, as Darian Leader observes in Chapter 3, is what is done with this sense of loss – whether it can figure as a loss at all.[7] Normal jealousy, then, is good not because it is a gain in itself, but because it is an indication of a gain – it is a leftover, an inevitable consequence, the *price* we must pay for encountering the world, indicating our receptivity to others, to their desire, and to their *reality*.

This of course involves losing one's fantasy, or at least its wholesale purchase on us. What is the fantasy we lose? We could call it a kind of love, a fantasy of total reciprocity, but we could also look at it through the prism of a perspective which is shattered – what is lost is a kind of knowingness, faith in understanding others and ourselves, which can sometimes occur too soon, meaning this loss is resisted. What differs between jealousies then, perhaps, is the management of the grief Freud noticed at the heart of the feeling. In projected jealousy, for reasons that are difficult to discern, there is a greater need for the illusion to be reconfigured, resulting in the person remaining in an undecided position with respect to what to do with the loss of imagined possession. It grieves the loss it perceives, but it also shores up that illusion elsewhere, short-circuiting the work of mourning – this refusal to give up on it altogether requires, then, that *it appears everywhere they are not*. All the while, they disavow this holding on: usually the pathologically jealous person thinks they '*just*' want reassurance of love, they are '*only*' insecure, and cannot detect the demand for devotion smuggled in to their '*not unreasonable*' requests. Yet, at some unconscious level, we can say jealousy is always ahead of the game: the reason the jealous demand devotion is surely bound up with the knowledge that devotion could *never* be offered unconditionally – unless it is a pretence! Hence the feeling of always having known, often accompanied with jealousy: *I knew it!* The jealous demands what cannot be met such that when it is not, a righteous suffering usurps what might otherwise be there. Grief, here, becomes grievance.

Yet in normal jealousy, too, there is a seeming regression to the imagined possession enjoyed by the infant. Winnicott observes that

> at first times of jealousy it is common for us to see children trying to revert to being infants, even if only in some way or for a little while. They may even want to re-experience a breast-feed. But commonly they long to just be treated as they were treated when they had full possession, when they were the ones who had, and they knew of no-one who had not, but wanted.

(p. 54)

It is not that the child *deludes* themselves into being the baby again; what they have come to recognise cannot be undone. Instead, they engage in an *illusion*, a little respite for a time, where they can enjoy what they imagine to have been this prior sense of having. My friend's son, despite his having achieved the capacity for new forms of curiosity and loving, perhaps through the help of his jealousy, still came downstairs for dinner in his little sister's new dress.

Isn't the infant's toying with illusion here quite close to the pleasures of monogamy? It is not that the couple believe themselves never to be wanting; rather, that they play at having and at being had – to love, as many a poet attests, is to play the fool. Does our contemporary distaste for monogamy say something about our lessoning capacity for playing, for enjoying the illusion for what it is? The attitude seems to have turned to something like: if we can't *really* possess our lovers (or we disagree with this on ethical grounds, which can sometimes be a contrary way to preserve the fantasy that this *could* be a reality), then why bother to play pretend? As though the only things worth having are things we can *really* have, things we can take into ourselves and permanently hold on to – which, well, rules out quite a lot of human experience. Or is it simply that what is played at has changed: perhaps the non-monogamous play at having possession over *themselves*, over their own desires, which could explain why this form of loving is so often linked to a 'finding' of the self.

In his essay 'Transitional Objects and Transitional Phenomena', D.W. Winnicott adds in a footnote to his subtitle, 'A Study of the First Not-Me Possession', that 'It is necessary to stress that the word used here is "possession" and not "object"', since when he accidently used the word 'object', there was the objection that the first 'not-me' object is the breast (1989, p. 89). Debate between differing British schools aside, we might add that there is another reason to highlight the dimension of *possession* in the transitional object; it is compensatory for the *non*-possession of the mother's love, for the giving up on this, the exchange of one illusion for another, somewhat self-created, one. It is notable that particularly jealous kids don't tend to take pleasure in a special little object of this kind – some piece of fabric which might be stroked by the child, say, or later graduating to a particular teddy. It may confuse them that other children should treat their possessions with such delicacy, and occur to them instead to want to puncture or destroy these silly illusions. Conversely, they may invest exclusively in possessions other children also want, since self-created not-me possessions do not come to develop an aura.

Winnicott thought that transitional phenomena constitute anything that delivers an illusion which the infant can hold on to, can possess; as such, it is neither just an externally provided nor just an internally created phenomenon, but both. Crucially, the function of this illusion for Winnicott is to support the infant's 'growing ability to recognize and accept reality', through allowing them an 'intermediate state' in which they are neither entirely shut off from nor solely engaged in that 'reality' (p. 90). If they were shut off, then all would still constitute 'Me', and, as becomes clear by the end of the essay, it is not possible for anyone to access 'reality' unfettered by the influence of our internal world. He explains,

> I am here staking a claim for an intermediate state between a baby's inability and growing ability to recognize and accept reality. I am therefore studying the substance of illusion, that which is allowed to the infant, and which in adult life is inherent in art and religion.

(p. 90)

Does normal or good jealousy not occupy a similarly liminal space? It offers up the illusion of possession at the same time as exposing us to its impossibility, in a painful way but also in a way which ushers in identificatory compensations: friendship, community. Jealousy here describes powerful disappointment that engenders a kind of 'same boatism', which can be turned to for genuine comfort even though it's not the original thing desired, much like the transitional object.

Perhaps, then, pathological jealousy dominates when disillusionment has been denied; where that intermediate, transitional space never subsequently overtook and instead, jealousy enacted its own kind of fantasy, instigating an equivalence between the inter- and intrapersonal. Many women trying to conceive talk about the difficulty they have managing feelings of envy (desiring what mothers have) and jealousy (feeling excluded from a realm of love which they long to be a part of), on top of the ongoing sense of grief in relation to their imagined future. What they have been denied, perhaps, is a chance to be disillusioned by motherhood, which is the same as saying a chance at creating their own version of it. They are in a way stuck in the realm of fantasy, taunted by their imagination, which has not yet had the opportunity of becoming replaced. This terrain – perhaps any terrain in which disillusionment is staved off – is ripe for jealousy.

For those who overlook that possession can only ever be played at, who are caught in enjoying projected jealousy, acute suffering is inevitable, since the upkeep requires constant vigilance and a never-ending cycle of grievance. 'Enjoy' is the right word only if we use it in the Lacanian sense, then. Since imagined possession always fails to materialise, there must be a fixation on *others* maintaining possession of what the subject feels rightfully entitled to. There is if you like a reconfiguration of the players, in order to sustain the illusion. Lacan gave this addictive enjoyment its own neologism: jalouissance.

Though Lacan doesn't exactly give us a definition, we could extrapolate that jalouissance describes the pleasure afforded by the painful belief that another possesses the object *a* and/or is the object *a* for the desired parent.[8] Even if the subject can never possess what they believe their rival does, by the same token a fantasy is sustained by 'seeing' or 'knowing' the rival has it. To put this sequentially, even if artificially: the pain of knowing such possession is impossible gives way to a jealous hatred which permits the subject to un-know this, by decreeing that it is them *alone* for whom this is impossible. Since this jealous hatred sustains a fantasy about the other's love being possessable, it begets both pleasure and pain. It's interesting here that the focus is generally on what the other *enjoys*, as Lacan was careful to note, rather than some other hidden morsel of experience. This shows us once again how jealousy collapses the I and the you, in a way which allows the subject to live vicariously through the other, but in an inverted way, in which they suffer the other's enjoyment (yet maintain a grip on its possibility).

Pursuing the other's enjoyment, the answers to jealous questions, embellishes, gives a landscape to, the unbridgeable void we face when we love others – which, the jealous subject wants not to know, is the distance needed for love to kindle into anything at all. All jealousy may be about wanting to know what cannot be known, then, but this projected jealousy adds a not wanting to know that it cannot.[9]

So jealousy is not *only* that which it appears to be, namely an *obstacle* to the social realm – a mechanism of control and a justification of spite – but also the gateway to that realm, perhaps our only gateway. It can, obviously, be dealt with very badly and contaminate everything in its path; but if the ignorance about the desires of others that normal jealousy exposes us to is reckoned with – the loss of our presumed knowledge and possession of it mourned – we get closer to an honest look at each other. An honest look here can only mean an ever-present grasp that there is always far more than meets the eye. As many couples' counsellors will tell you, giving this dignity back to the beloved can and often does, ironically, give subjects something of what cannot be possessed: they receive what cannot be given, to invert Lacan's formula for love.[10] Or, as Rainer Maria Rilke put it: 'the highest task for a bond between two people [is for] each [to protect] the solitude of the other. This is the miracle that happens every time to those who really love: the more they give, the more they possess' (1929, p. 22).

Jealousy is described by thinkers in a diverse range of fields as a social emotion – it arises out of our encounters with other people. Because of this, it is not enough to say jealousy raises ethical questions: ethical considerations pertaining to the smudged line between I and you and the freedoms we each want to vouchsafe, in many ways *define* the feeling. It can, as this chapter has tried to highlight, function to *support* the social, even be necessary to it; but it can also function to support the subject to renounce the social, becoming a powerful weapon in the armoury of the asocial. But, if we're being optimists, how to return from the second function back to the first? As a culture, are we too far gone, is it a matter of unpicking individual histories of trauma, as Mitchell suggests in *Fratriarchy* (2023), highlighting the singularity of the sibling trauma and its links to misogyny? Or can an attitude of not knowing others be collectively re-found, out of which a genuine curiosity, as opposed to a paranoid surveillance, might emerge?

Despite admirable attempts to exact and avoid instances of oppression, both as a society and in our personal relationships, contemporary solutions tend to oversimplify the terrain of relationships by proclaiming that some peoples' freedoms need reigning in for others' to be less infringed upon. Putting aside the problem that this approach is easily perverted by whomever cries victim – we've seen it taken up by people who already harness power – this approach smuggles in a presumption that distinctions between people are clear and delineable, which itself harnesses an illusion about self and other possession. Which is to say, we have traded in the complexity of other people for known and trespassing others. This seems to have allowed us to neglect our most fundamental duty to others, even whilst we try to vouchsafe their freedom: looking them in the eye.

Notes

1   Sianne Ngai makes this argument in *Ugly Feelings* (2005), when she observes that the positive object of envy is *equality*.

2 'What do you think of jealousy? Is it good or bad? Normal or abnormal?', D.W. Winnicott asks (2017, 53). It is as if the third question follows from the difficulty answering
   the second – Freud too, short of being able to defend or denounce jealousy, ends up
   arguing that it is ordinary (despite leading to some quite extraordinary behaviours).
3 See Chapter 1, this volume.
4 He is not conclusive, but suggests jealousy proper is rarely seen before a baby is 15
   months old.
5 Though 'mother' traditionally identifies a feminine subject, I am using it more here to
   describe an attachment, and as a verb – male relatives, grandparents, godparents, and so
   on can also mother if they are primary caregiver.
6 Though we might question the idea of the mother's 'agency' here, which doesn't exactly
   arrive suddenly but continues to be wrestled with well into adulthood. Arguably, our
   mothers are subjects whose realness can never quite materialise for us, or only ever in
   glimpses, so invested are we in their status as psychic objects.
7 'The tempering effects of this process [of the Lacanian Oedipus] revolve around the
   inscription of a signification of loss', Leader writes. What I am calling 'good' jealousy
   is a side effect of this process of inscribing oedipal losses; it is if you like the pain that
   comes with that process of signification, it is a feeling which resists, which ekes out the
   very last remainder of hope before disappointment commemorates loss.
8 Lacan asks in Seminar XX: 'the child who is gazed at [by Saint Augustine] has it – he
   has the *a*. Is having the *a* the same as being it? That is the question with which I will
   leave you today' (1988, p. 100). It is a question he will try to develop, but for our purposes we can say that both evoke 'jalouissance'. We might even add that the transition
   from attempting to possess the object *a* to managing somehow to *be* the object *a* marks
   the moment of disillusionment which the terribly jealous subject fails to experience,
   hence their staying so caught up in possession.
9 A step further into this commitment to not knowing would of course be delusional jealousy, in which this was never known, but foreclosed.
10 'Love is giving what you don't have' (2015, p. 34).

Reference list

Elkin, L. (2024). *Scaffolding*. Vintage Books.
Freud, S. (1922). Some neurotic mechanisms in paranoia, jealousy and homosexuality.
   In *Standard edition* (Vol. 18, pp. 221–232). The Hogarth Press.
Klein, M. (1975). *Envy and gratitude and other works 1946–1963* (M. Khan, Ed.). The
   International Psycho-Analytical Library.
Lacan, J. (1988). *Encore, the seminar of Jacques Lacan Book XX: On female sexuality,
   the limits of love and knowledge, 1972–1973* (B. Fink, Trans.). Norton. (Original work
   published 1975)
Lacan, J. (2015). *Transference: The seminar of Jacques Lacan book VIII* (B. Fink, Trans.). Polity.
Mitchell, J. (2023). *Fratriarchy: The sibling trauma and the law of the mother*. Routledge.
Ngai, S. (2005). *Ugly feelings*. Harvard University Press.
Ogden, E. (2022). *On not knowing: How to love and other essays*. University of Chicago Press.
Rilke, R.M. (2002). *Letters to a young poet* (R. Snell Trans.). Dover Publications. (Original
   work published 1929).
Riviere, J. (1932). Jealousy as a mechanism of defence. *International Journal of Psychoa-
   nalysis*, *13*, 414–424.
Winnicott, D.W. (1989). Transitional objects and transitional phenomena – a study of the
   first not-me possession. *The International Journal of Psycho-Analysis*, *34*, 89–97.
Winnicott, D.W. (2017). Jealousy. In L. Caldwell & H. Taylor Robinson (Eds.), *The collected
   works of D. W. Winnicott. Vol. 6, 1960–3* (pp. 46–63). (Original work published 1960).

For Product Safety Concerns and Information please contact our EU
representative GPSR@taylorandfrancis.com
Taylor & Francis Verlag GmbH, Kaufingerstraße 24, 80331 München, Germany

www.ingramcontent.com/pod-product-compliance
Lightning Source LLC
Chambersburg PA
CBHW050617280326
41932CB00016B/3081

9 781032 637501